CW01376667

MENUS

GOOD FOOD, GREAT TIMES

BAUER
MEDIA GROUP

PUBLISHED IN 2016 BY *AUSTRALIAN GOURMET TRAVELLER*,
IN CONJUNCTION WITH BAUER MEDIA BOOKS, AUSTRALIA.
AUSTRALIAN GOURMET TRAVELLER AND BAUER MEDIA BOOKS
ARE PUBLISHED BY BAUER MEDIA PTY LTD.

AUSTRALIAN GOURMET TRAVELLER
Editor Anthea Loucas Bosha
Deputy Editor Pat Nourse
Art Director Anna Vu
Food & Style Director Emma Knowles
Senior Food Editor Lisa Featherby
Food Editor-at-Large Alice Storey
Contributing Food Editors Nick Banbury,
Rodney Dunn and Brigitte Hafner
Chief Subeditor Toni Mason

BAUER MEDIA BOOKS
Publisher Jo Runciman
Director of Sales, Marketing & Rights Brian Cearnes

A catalogue record for this book is available from
the National Library of Australia.
ISBN 978-1742458762 (hardback)
© Bauer Media Pty Limited 2016
ABN 18 053 273 546
This publication is copyright. No part of it may be
reproduced or transmitted in any form without the
written permission of the publishers.

Printed in China by Leo Paper Products Ltd

BAUER MEDIA BOOKS IS A DIVISION
OF BAUER MEDIA PTY LTD.
54 Park St, Sydney; GPO Box 4088;
Sydney, NSW 2001, Australia
Ph +61 2 9282 8618; Fax +61 2 9126 3702

Chief Executive Officer Nick Chan
Publisher – Specialist Division Cornelia Schulze

To order books phone 136 116 (within Australia)
or order online at magshop.com.au

GOURMET
TRAVELLER

MENUS

GOOD FOOD, GREAT TIMES

OUR FAVOURITE RECIPES TO SHARE WITH FRIENDS

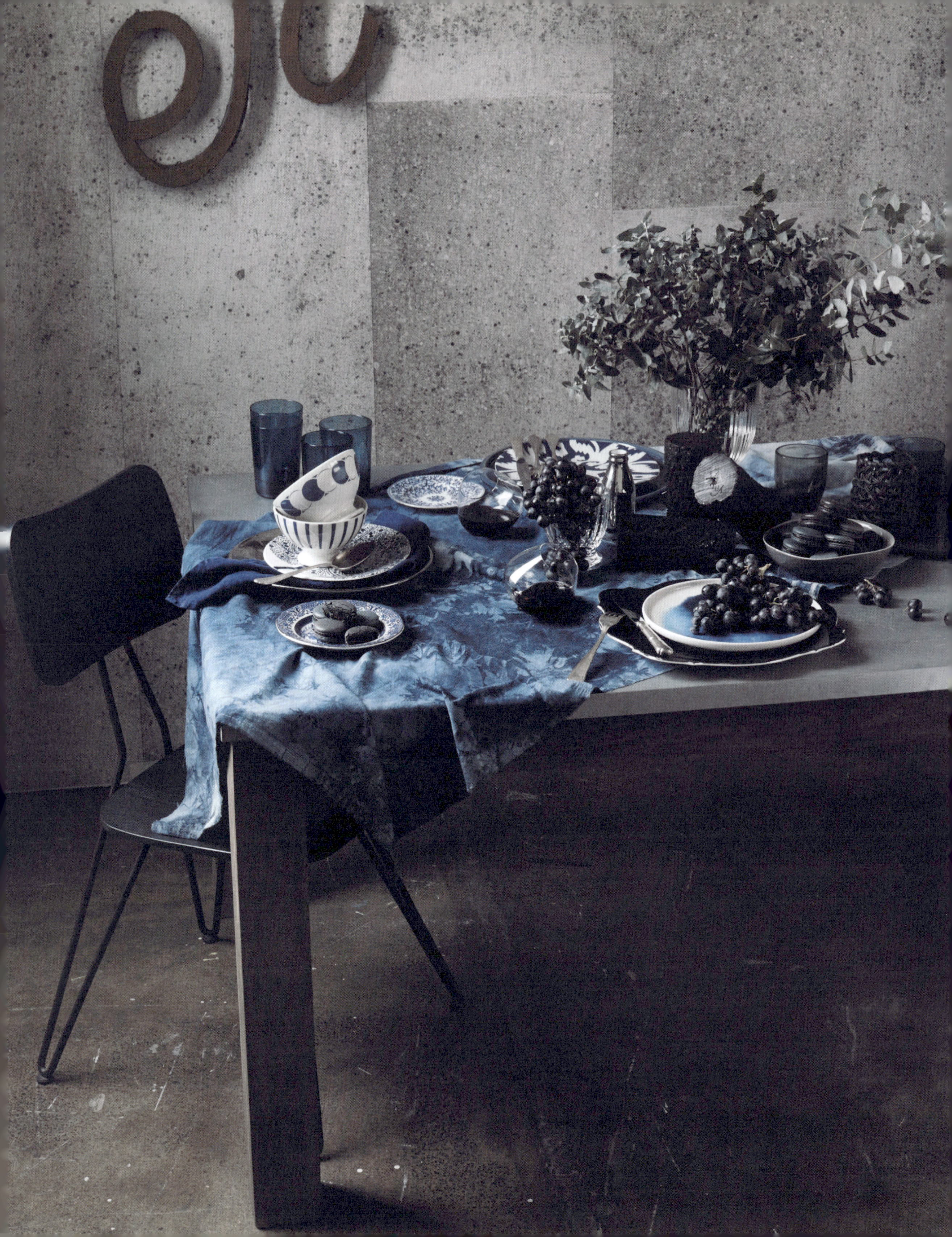

CONTENTS

INTRODUCTION 9

BONDI CLAMBAKE
10

CHRISTMAS FEAST
30

LUNCH BY THE BEACH
48

HOLLYWOOD DINNER PARTY
64

SMART-CASUAL LUNCH
82

LUNCH IN PARIS
98

CHRISTMAS ALFRESCO
120

EASTER AT ESTER
136

LEE HO FOOK'S ASIAN BANQUET
154

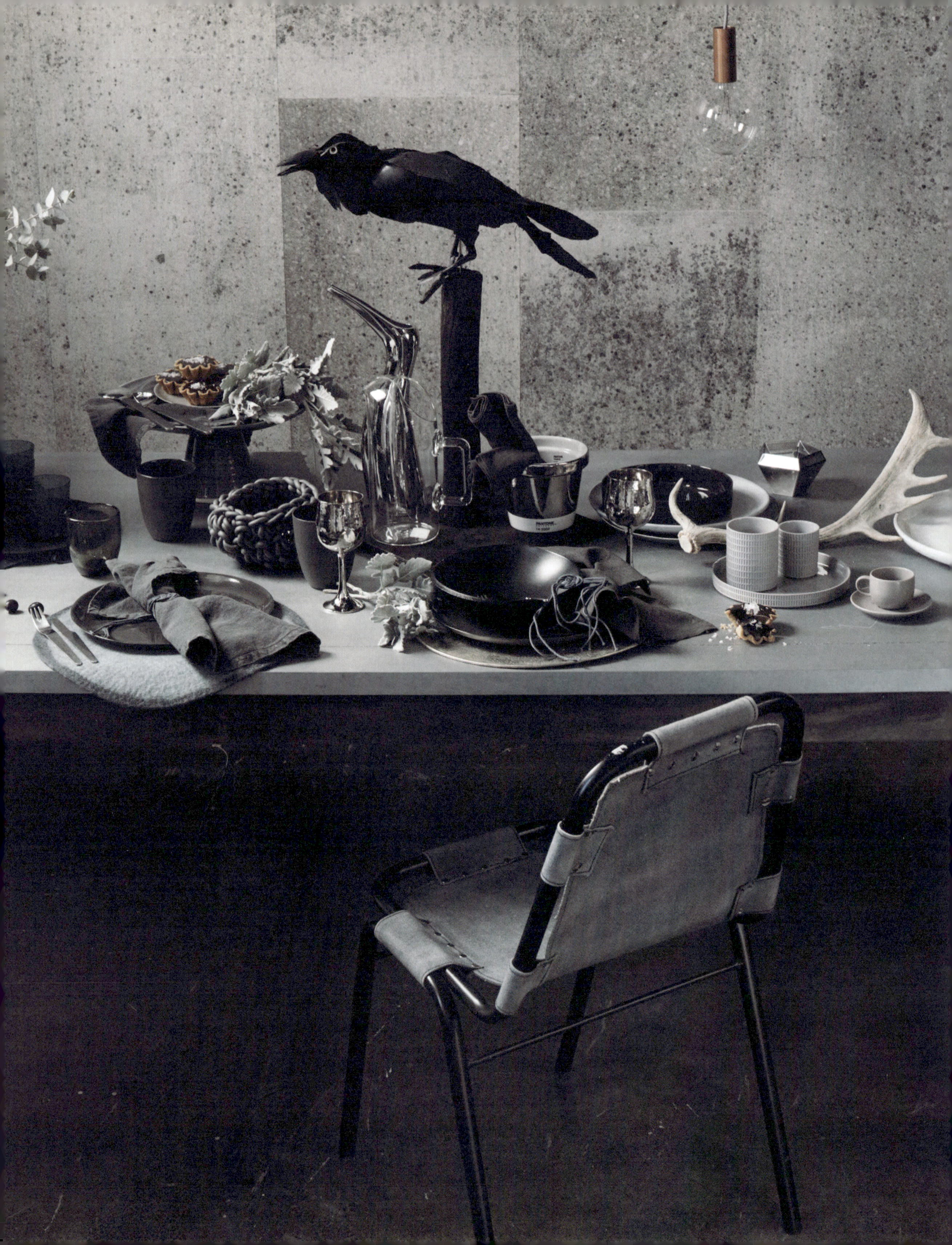

CONTENTS

BLUE MOUNTAINS
HARVEST LUNCH

170

EASTER AT
10 WILLIAM ST

186

FIRESIDE SUPPER

204

SUNDAY LUNCH WITH
PETER GILMORE

220

APRÈS-SKI WITH THE
THREE BLUE DUCKS

242

COCKTAIL HOUR

258

INDEX **272**

COOK'S NOTES **279**

ACKNOWLEDGEMENTS **280**

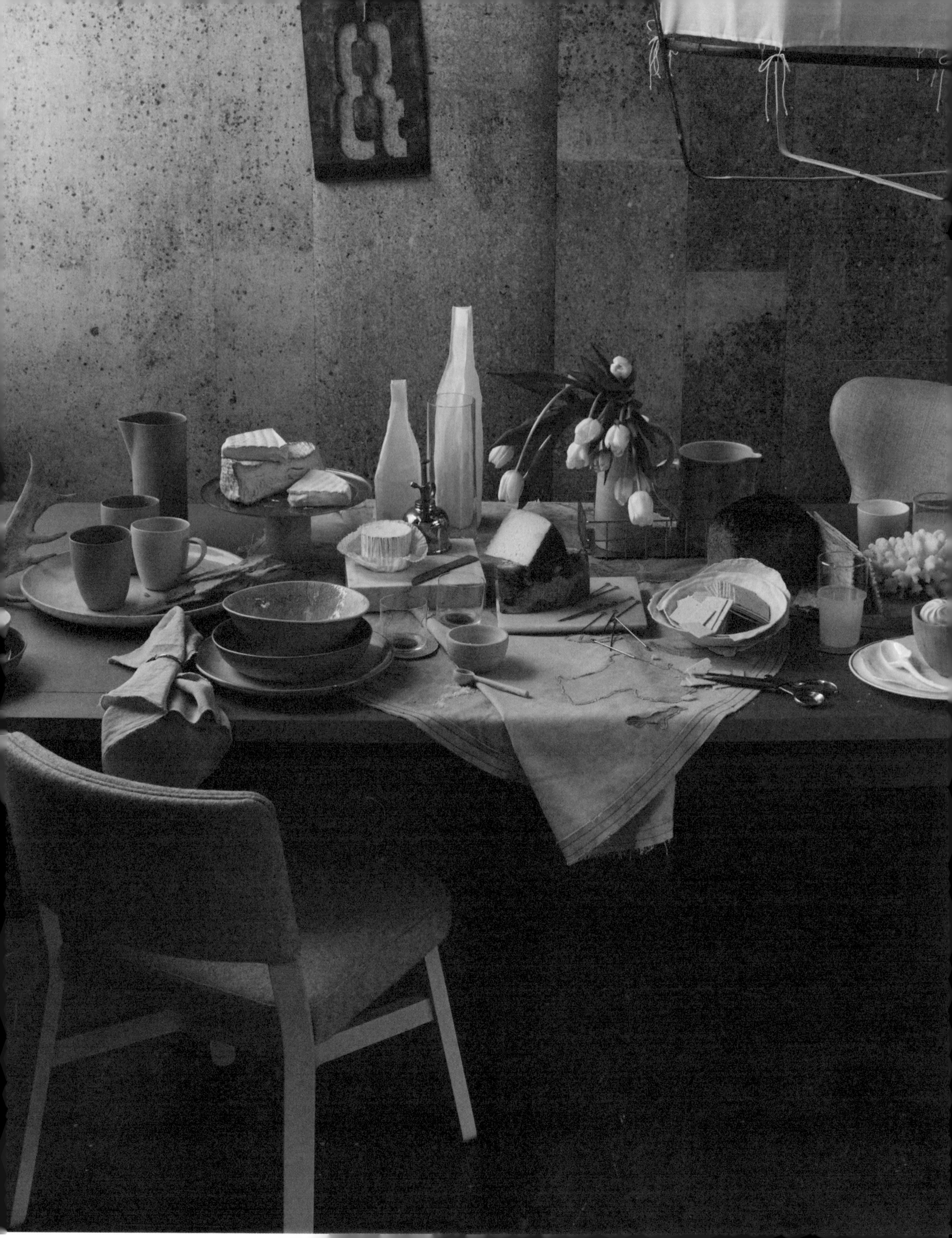

INTRODUCTION

At Gourmet Traveller *we've been sharing food inspiration with Australian cooks for more than 50 years. And while we've published thousands of recipes and hundreds of cooking tips, the most important ingredient of any meal is the company. Gathering your nearest and dearest around the table is what the enjoyment of good food is all about and to cook for people you love is a gift that's always welcome. It's with this in mind that we chose to make our first hardcover cookbook a collection of menus. Good food brings people together, whether you're lunching in Paris or feasting in the snow, whether you're supping fireside or snacking by the beach, whether it's Christmas or Easter or any other festive occasion in between – and good times are the result. These are some of our favourite recipes – we hope you enjoy sharing them with your family and friends as much as we enjoy sharing them with you.*

–

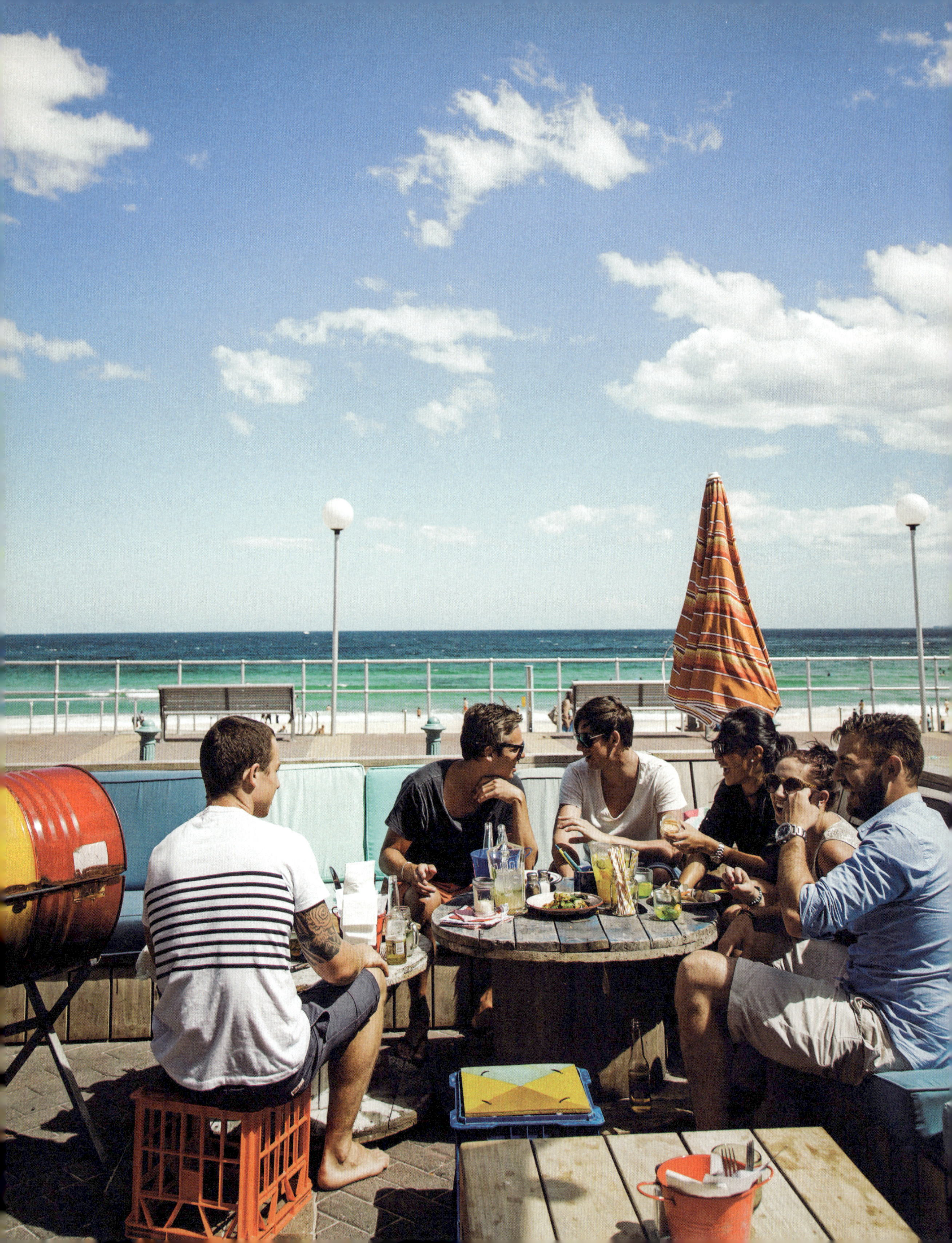

BONDI CLAMBAKE

The New England-style clambake comes to Bondi Beach with this menu from chef Tom Walton of The Bucket List, replete with drawn butter, chowder and all the trimmings. Just add sun and surf.

—

+ Dark and Stormy

+ Clam chowder

+ Char-grilled corn

+ Tomato salad with feta and basil

+ Sautéed zucchini flowers with lemon, chilli and garlic

+ Clambake

+ Blueberry cobbler with lemon curd cream

—

DARK AND STORMY

"The ginger syrup keeps in a sterilised jar or bottle in the refrigerator for up to a month, so I make it in large quantities to have on hand in the summer," says Tom Walton. "It's the perfect hot-weather drink."

SERVES 6-8

—

180 ml dark rum (Walton uses Kraken Black Spiced Rum)
1 cup (firmly packed) mint leaves
2 lemons, thinly sliced
Ice and soda water, to serve

GINGER SYRUP
75 gm ginger, peeled and coarsely chopped
250 gm caster sugar
125 ml ($\frac{1}{2}$ cup) lemon juice
15 gm runny honey
$\frac{1}{2}$ long red chilli, seeded, coarsely chopped
500 ml (2 cups) filtered water

1 For ginger syrup, process ingredients in a blender until smooth, strain through a muslin-lined sieve and refrigerate in a sterilised container (see cook's notes p279) until required. Makes 1 litre.

2 Combine 250ml ginger syrup in a jug with rum, mint and lemon, and use a rolling pin or muddler to muddle briefly. Top up with ice and soda water to taste and serve.

BONDI CLAMBAKE

BONDI CLAMBAKE

CLAM CHOWDER

"Storm clams are larger sweet clams that are perfect for this chowder," says Walton. "While this soup is rich with its cream component, the anise flavour of the fennel and the tarragon really freshens things up."

PREP TIME 10 MINS, COOK 30 MINS
SERVES 6-8

- 1 kg Cloudy Bay storm clams, or other large clams
- 60 gm unsalted butter, coarsely chopped
- 1 leek, finely chopped
- 1 fennel bulb, finely chopped
- 2 garlic cloves, finely chopped
- 200 ml dry white wine
- 500 ml (2 cups) fish stock
- 500 ml (2 cups) pouring cream
- 2 large King Edward potatoes, cut into 1cm dice
- 150 gm podded broad beans (about 350gm unpodded)
- ⅔ cup coarsely chopped French tarragon
- 2 tbsp coarsely chopped dill
- Juice of 1 lemon
- Crusty bread, to serve

1 Heat a large saucepan over medium heat, add clams, cover with a tight-fitting lid and cook, shaking pan occasionally, until clams open (3-4 minutes). Remove from heat, then, when cool enough to handle, remove meat from shells (reserve a few in shells to serve; discard remaining shells), finely chop and set aside, reserving pan juices separately.

2 Melt butter in a medium saucepan over low heat, add leek, fennel and garlic and sauté, stirring occasionally, until softened but not coloured (4-5 minutes). Add wine, simmer until reduced by half (2-3 minutes), then add stock and reserved clam juices and simmer until reduced by half (5-7 minutes). Add cream and potato, and simmer until potato is just tender and chowder thickens slightly (8-10 minutes).

3 Meanwhile, blanch broad beans until just tender (1-2 minutes; see cook's notes p279), refresh, peel and add to chowder along with herbs, lemon juice and chopped clams. Top with reserved clams in shells and serve hot with crusty bread.

DRINK SUGGESTION American-style pale ale.

16 GOURMET TRAVELLER | MENUS

TOM WALTON

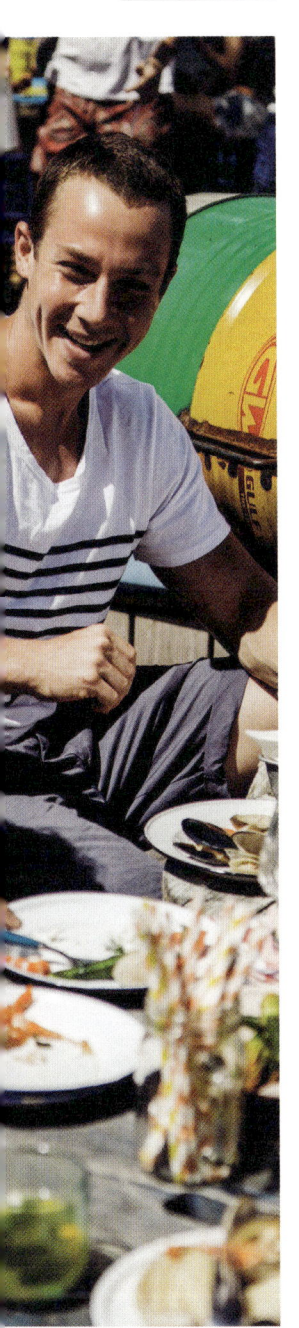

BONDI CLAMBAKE

CHAR-GRILLED CORN

PREP TIME 10 MINS, COOK 15 MINS (PLUS SOAKING)
SERVES 6-8

—

8 corn cobs, husks on
120 gm butter, melted
Lemon wedges and smoked paprika, to serve

1 Peel back husks of corn and remove silk. Pull husks back over to cover corn, then soak in a large bowl of cold water for 20 minutes to prevent scorching. Meanwhile, heat a charcoal barbecue to high heat. Drain corn, then grill corn over hot coals, turning occasionally, until charred and tender (10-15 minutes). Serve hot drizzled with butter and a squeeze of lemon, and scattered with smoked paprika and sea salt to taste.
DRINK SUGGESTION Australian-style pale ale.

BONDI CLAMBAKE

BONDI CLAMBAKE

TOMATO SALAD WITH FETA AND BASIL

PREP TIME 10 MINS
SERVES 6-8

—

6 ripe oxheart tomatoes, cut into wedges
120 gm marinated feta, crumbled
50 ml extra-virgin olive oil
1 tbsp red wine vinegar
Finely grated rind and juice of ½ lemon
Finely chopped basil, plus leaves, to serve

1 Arrange tomatoes and feta on a platter. Whisk oil, vinegar, and lemon rind and juice in a bowl to combine, drizzle dressing over tomatoes, season to taste and serve scattered with basil.

SAUTÉED ZUCCHINI FLOWERS WITH
LEMON, CHILLI AND GARLIC

CLAMBAKE

BONDI CLAMBAKE

SAUTÉED ZUCCHINI FLOWERS WITH LEMON, CHILLI AND GARLIC

PREP TIME 15 MINS, COOK 5 MINS
SERVES 6-8

—

90 ml extra-virgin olive oil
24 female zucchini flowers, trimmed, stamens removed
⅓ cup (firmly packed) finely chopped flat-leaf parsley
1½ birdseye chillies, finely chopped
1½ garlic cloves, finely chopped
Juice of 1½ lemons
Pea shoots or micro-cress, to serve

1 Heat oil in a large frying pan over medium-high heat, add zucchini flowers, season to taste and fry, stirring occasionally, until wilted (2 minutes). Add parsley, chilli and garlic, toss to combine and warm through (1 minute), then add lemon juice. Season to taste and serve warm or at room temperature topped with pea shoots or micro-cress.

CLAMBAKE

"The secret to a great clambake lies in the quality of the seafood and the company you share it with," says Walton. A traditional clambake is cooked in a firepit lined with sea stones and seaweed, although Walton cooks his in a coal barbecue. You can also cook the seafood bundles on a rack placed over a heatproof bowl filled with water in a kettle barbecue. Potatoes roasted among the hot coals make the perfect accompaniment to this dish. Choose small potatoes, wrap them individually in foil and place them in the coals when you add the sea stones.

PREP TIME 35 MINS, COOK 30 MINS
SERVES 6-8

- 48 Cloudy Bay diamond-shell clams, or other small clams
- 24 Cloudy Bay tuatua clams, or other clams
- 40 mussels, scrubbed and beards removed
- 16 uncooked tiger prawns
- 3 lemons, thinly sliced
- 8 thyme sprigs

POTATO AÏOLI
- 150 gm sebago potato, peeled and diced
- 2 egg yolks
- 10 gm garlic, finely grated on a Microplane
- 250 ml (1 cup) grapeseed oil
- 125 ml (½ cup) extra-virgin olive oil
- Lemon juice, to taste

MARIE ROSE SAUCE
- 200 gm mayonnaise
- 50 gm ketchup
- 1 tbsp Worcestershire sauce
- 10 ml brandy
- Tabasco sauce, to taste
- Lemon juice, to taste

DRAWN BUTTER
- 200 gm unsalted butter, coarsely chopped
- ¼ cup finely chopped flat-leaf parsley
- 2 tbsp lemon juice
- 1 garlic clove, finely chopped

1 For potato aïoli, cover potato in a saucepan with plenty of cold water, bring to the boil and cook until tender (8-10 minutes). Drain well, pass through a ricer or coarse sieve and keep hot. Whisk yolks and garlic in a separate bowl to combine, then mix in hot potato. Whisking continuously, add the combined oils in a thin steady stream until thick and emulsified (thin with a little hot water if the mixture gets too thick). Season to taste with lemon juice, sea salt and freshly ground black pepper and refrigerate until required.

2 For Marie Rose sauce, combine ingredients in a bowl, season to taste with lemon juice, sea salt and freshly ground black pepper and refrigerate until required.

3 Build a fire in a kettle barbecue using hardwood logs or charcoal. Once fire has burnt down, place sea stones among the hot coals and leave for an hour to get very hot (add more wood or charcoal if necessary).

4 Meanwhile, cut eight 40cm squares of muslin and place on a work surface. Divide clams, mussels, prawns, lemon and thyme sprigs evenly among muslin squares, season to taste and tie into pouches with kitchen string (ensure string isn't plastic-coated or it will melt). Refrigerate until required.

5 When the rocks are red-hot, place some wet seaweed on them, then arrange the pouches on top. Cover with a potato sack or pillowcase soaked in beer or water. Close lid and cook until clams open and prawns are opaque (35-40 minutes).

6 Meanwhile, for drawn butter, cook butter in a saucepan over medium-high heat until milk solids separate and are slightly caramelised on the bottom of the pan to create a slight nutty flavour (6-7 minutes). Strain the butter into a heatproof bowl, add remaining ingredients, season to taste and keep warm.

7 Serve the seafood pouches hot with scissors for cutting them open, and potato aïoli, Marie Rose sauce and drawn butter.

WINE SUGGESTION Chilled, pale, dry rosé.

BLUEBERRY COBBLER WITH LEMON CURD CREAM

"The classic cobbler is ideal for entertaining – most of the work can be done several hours ahead," says Walton. "You can use any seasonal fruit – a mix of berries or stone fruit works well."

PREP TIME 30 MINS, COOK 45 MINS (PLUS CHILLING)
SERVES 6-8

—

- 250 gm (1⅔ cups) plain flour
- ½ tsp baking powder
- 80 gm unsalted butter, at room temperature
- 220 gm (1 cup) caster sugar
- 2 eggs, lightly whisked
- 125 ml (½ cup) buttermilk
- 1 kg blueberries (about 8 punnets)
- 1 tbsp dark rum
- Scraped seeds of ½ vanilla bean
- 1 tsp ground cinnamon
- Pure icing sugar, for dusting
- Vanilla ice-cream, to serve

LEMON CURD CREAM
- 5 egg yolks
- 110 ml lemon juice
- 100 gm caster sugar
- 125 gm chilled unsalted butter, diced
- 250 ml (1 cup) thickened cream, whisked to soft peaks

1 For lemon curd cream, whisk yolks, lemon juice and sugar in a heatproof bowl over a saucepan of simmering water until thick and pale (4-5 minutes). Remove from heat, then whisk in butter a piece at a time until mixture is thick and emulsified. Transfer to a clean bowl, refrigerate until well chilled, then fold in cream and refrigerate until required.

2 Preheat oven to 180C. Sieve 240gm flour and baking powder into a bowl and set aside. Beat butter and 150gm caster sugar in an electric mixer until light and fluffy (4-5 minutes), scraping down sides of bowl occasionally. Gradually add egg, beating to combine, then add 30gm of the flour mixture and beat to combine. Add buttermilk, then remaining flour mixture and beat until smooth. Set aside.

3 Combine blueberries, rum, vanilla seeds, 50gm caster sugar and remaining flour in a separate bowl, then spoon into a 1.75-litre ovenproof dish and dollop batter on top. Combine cinnamon and remaining caster sugar in a small bowl, scatter on top of cobbler and bake until golden and a skewer inserted into the batter withdraws clean (35-40 minutes). Dust with icing sugar and serve warm with lemon curd cream and vanilla ice-cream.

WINE SUGGESTION Refreshing sherbety moscato.

BONDI CLAMBAKE

28 GOURMET TRAVELLER | MENUS

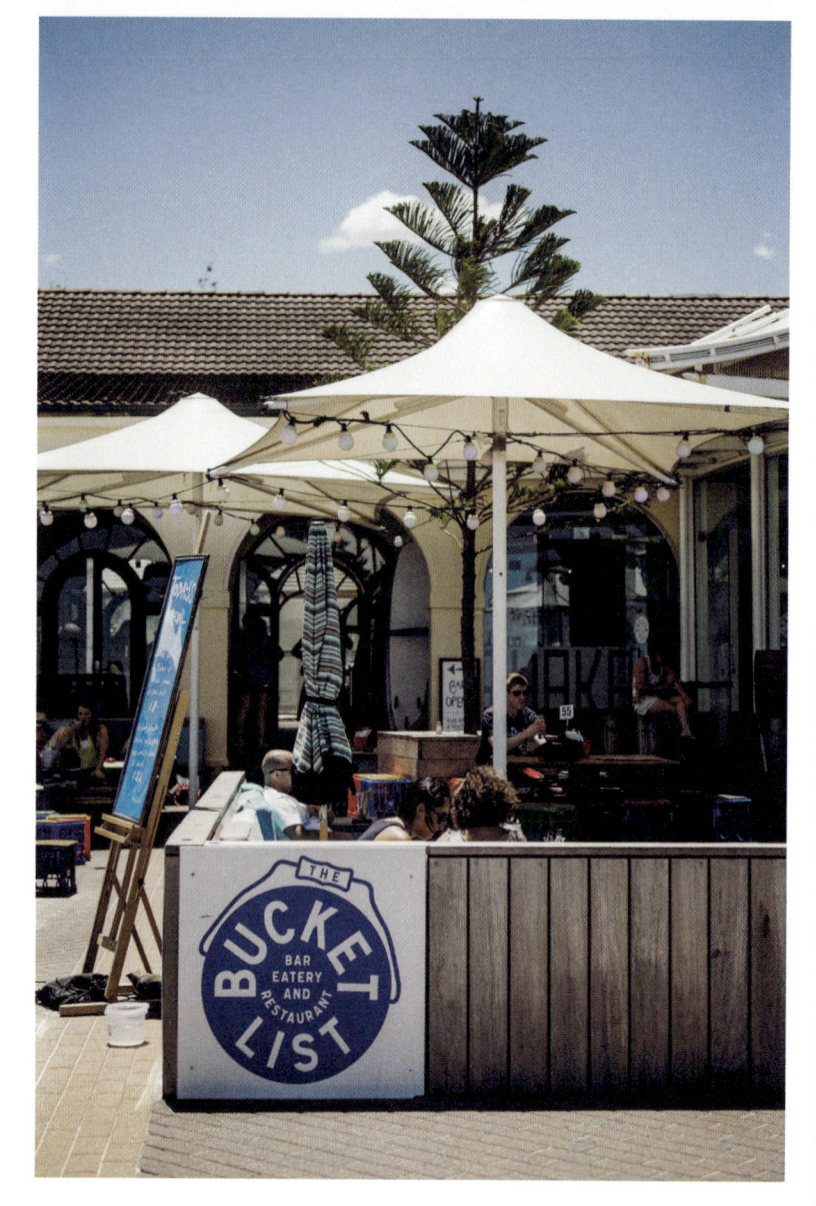

BONDI CLAMBAKE

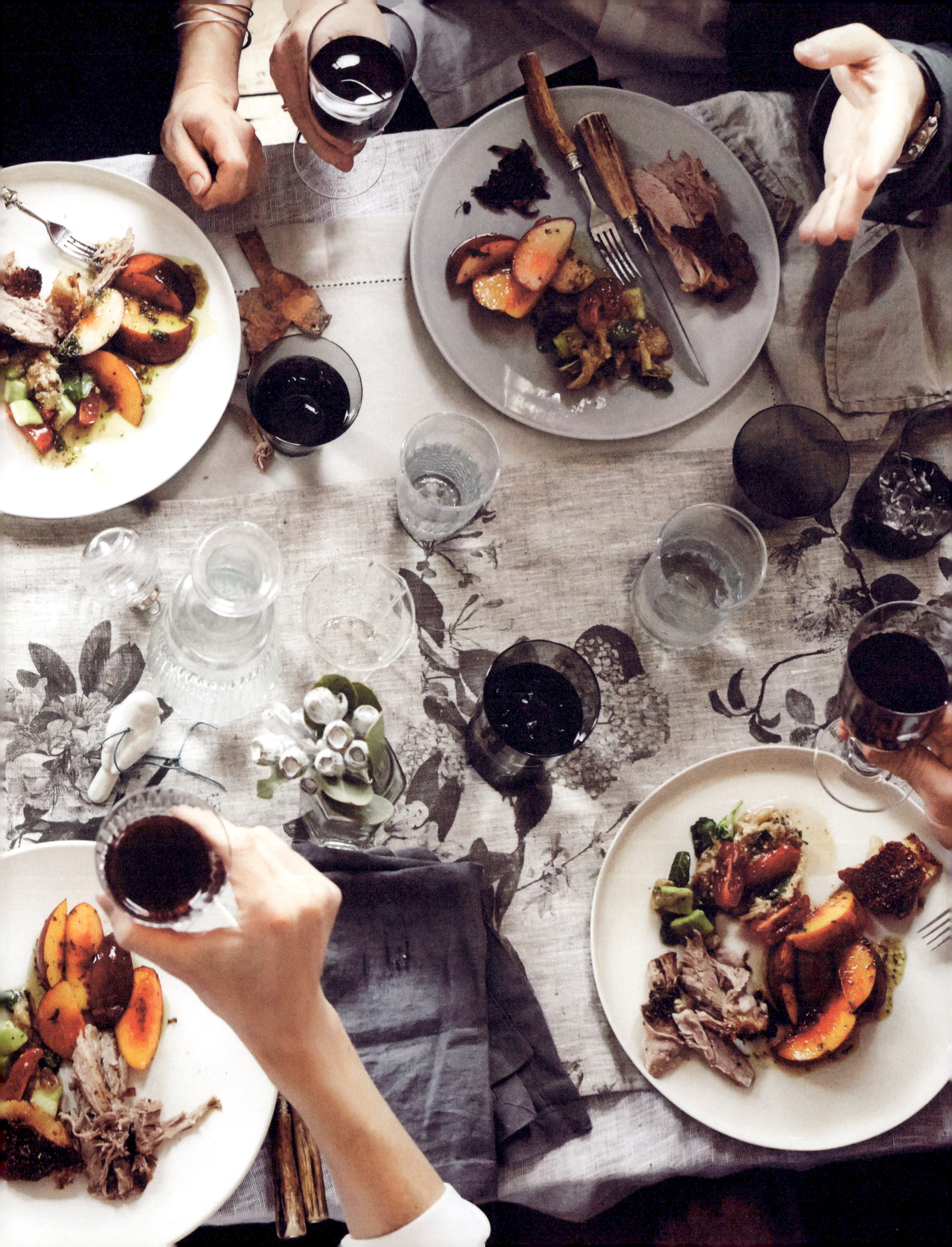

CHRISTMAS FEAST

There's more to Christmas than roast turkey, as this culture-crossing menu demonstrates, from spicy lamb cigars to lobster tagliarini and the best-ever roast pork. With recipes by chef Brigitte Hafner, the team at Melbourne's Gertrude Street Enoteca celebrate the special day in rare style.

—

+ Enoteca Tonic

+ Crostini with smoked eel pâté and glacé beetroot

+ Spicy lamb cigars in brik pastry

+ Lobster tagliarini

+ Roast shoulder of pork

+ Smoky eggplant and pomegranate salad

+ Nectarine salad

+ Chocolate and Turkish coffee granita with poached cherries

—

ENOTECA TONIC

"We came up with this cocktail because we were excited about two interesting winemakers branching out to make these fantastic spirits," says Brigitte Hafner. *"Melbourne Gin Company Dry Gin by Andrew Marks, and the other a semi-dry vermouth using Australian botanicals called Maidenii Classic, from Sutton Grange winemaker Gilles Lapalus."*

PREP TIME 10 MINS, COOK 10 MINS
MAKES 8

- 250 ml Maidenii Classic medium-dry vermouth (see note)
- 125 ml (½ cup) Fever-Tree tonic water
- 60 ml Melbourne Gin Company gin
- 125 ml (½ cup) sugar syrup (see note)
- 1 tsp rose water
- 250 ml (1 cup) pink grapefruit juice, chilled

CANDIED ORANGE PEEL
- Thinly peeled rind of 1 orange, pith removed, cut into julienne
- 110 gm (⅓ cup) caster sugar

1 For candied orange peel, blanch rind (1 minute; see cook's notes p279), then combine in a saucepan with sugar and 50ml water, and simmer over medium heat until peel is transparent and candied (6-8 minutes). Set aside to cool.

2 Combine cocktail ingredients in a large jug and stir, then pour into chilled glasses over ice, garnish with candied peel and serve.

NOTE Maidenii Classic vermouth is available from select bottle shops. To make sugar syrup, bring 90gm caster sugar and 80ml water to the boil in a small saucepan, stirring to dissolve, then cool. Makes 130ml.

CHRISTMAS FEAST

CHRISTMAS FEAST

CROSTINI WITH SMOKED EEL PÂTÉ AND GLACÉ BEETROOT

"This eel pâté is delicate, rich and moreish," says Hafner. "It goes well with just about any drink and can be made a few days ahead of serving."

PREP TIME 25 MINS, COOK 30 MINS (PLUS COOLING)
MAKES 24

—

1 sourdough baguette, thinly sliced
80 ml (⅓ cup) extra-virgin olive oil

SMOKED EEL PÂTÉ
40 gm butter, coarsely chopped
2 tbsp extra-virgin olive oil
4 golden shallots, thinly sliced
1 smoked eel (450gm), skinned, boned, coarsely flaked
3 thyme sprigs
150 ml dry white wine
250 gm crème fraîche

GLACÉ BEETROOT
250 gm caster sugar
250 ml (1 cup) balsamic vinegar
2 tsp whole allspice
2 tsp black peppercorns
1 cinnamon quill
1 medium beetroot (190gm), peeled, thinly sliced on a mandolin into rounds

1 For smoked eel pâté, heat butter and oil in a deep frying pan over medium heat, add shallot and sauté, stirring occasionally, until pale golden (5-6 minutes). Add eel, thyme and salt to taste (be careful; smoked eel is salty), then stir until eel starts to brown (2-3 minutes). Turn up heat to medium-high and deglaze pan with white wine, simmering until reduced by half (3-5 minutes). Remove from heat, transfer to a bowl and refrigerate to cool (45 minutes). Discard thyme, then pulse mixture in a food processor until smooth. Whip crème fraîche in a bowl until soft peaks form, then fold into eel mixture. Check seasoning and refrigerate until required. Smoked eel pâté will keep for 4 days in the fridge.

2 For glacé beetroot, combine sugar, vinegar and spices in a saucepan and bring to the boil, then simmer over medium heat until reduced by a quarter (10 minutes). Strain into a clean pan, discarding spices. Add beetroot to liquid and gently simmer over medium heat until beetroot is tender and slightly sticky (10-15 minutes). This can be prepared a few days in advance; refrigerate in a sealed plastic container. When ready to serve, drain beetroot on paper towels.

3 Preheat oven to 220C. Place baguette slices on oven trays, drizzle with oil and toast in the oven, turning once, until golden on both sides (8-10 minutes). Cool completely. Crostini will keep in a sealed container for up to 2 days.

4 To serve, scoop the eel pâté onto crostini and top with a slice of glacé beetroot.

WINE SUGGESTION A sparkling rosé.

LEFT: SPICY LAMB CIGARS IN BRIK PASTRY

SPICY LAMB CIGARS IN BRIK PASTRY

"I fry these – I find the result is crunchier – but they can also be cooked in a hot oven if brushed with olive oil," says Hafner. "I prefer to cook the minced lamb when it's fresh, but the mixture can be made in advance."

PREP TIME 15 MINS, COOK 20 MINS (PLUS COOLING)
MAKES 16

—

- 1 tbsp olive oil
- 20 gm butter
- 1 onion, finely chopped
- 2 tsp cumin seeds, dry-roasted and ground (see cook's notes p279)
- 1 tsp whole allspice, finely ground
- ½ tsp sweet paprika
- 300 gm coarsely minced lamb
- 2 tbsp coarsely chopped flat-leaf parsley
- 16 sheets brik pastry (240gm, about 1½ packets; see note)
- 2 egg yolks, lightly beaten
- Vegetable oil, for deep-frying

1 Heat olive oil and butter in a saucepan, add onion and sauté over low heat, stirring occasionally, until softened and golden (12-15 minutes). Add spices and cook until fragrant (1 minute), then increase heat to medium-high, add lamb and salt to taste, and fry gently, stirring continuously and breaking up clumps with a wooden spoon, until lamb is cooked but not browned – it should be juicy and smell sweet (3-4 minutes). Set aside to cool (the mixture can be prepared in advance up to this stage), then add parsley and season to taste.

2 Trim brik pastry to 11cm x 15cm rectangles. Place a heaped tablespoonful of lamb mixture along the length of a pastry rectangle, leaving 2cm at each end, brush the edges with egg yolk, then tuck in sides and roll into a cigar shape. Set aside covered with a damp tea towel and repeat with remaining pastry and lamb.

3 Heat oil in a large, deep saucepan to 180C and deep-fry cigars until brown and crisp (2-3 minutes; take care, hot oil will spit). Drain on paper towels and serve.

NOTE Brik pastry is available from Middle Eastern grocers.
WINE SUGGESTION A sparkling rosé.

BRIGITTE HAFNER

CHRISTMAS FEAST

LOBSTER TAGLIARINI

"It's impressive to have lobster on the menu," says Hafner, "and the great thing with a pasta dish like this is that a little lobster goes a long way. It also works well with good dried pasta if you don't want to make your own – I recommend Benedetto Cavalieri spaghetti from Simon Johnson."

PREP TIME 45 MINS, COOK 20 MINS (PLUS STANDING)
SERVES 8

—

- 2 small live lobsters (about 450gm each)
- 50 gm butter, diced
- 125 ml (½ cup) extra-virgin olive oil, plus extra for sauce if necessary
- 2 small garlic cloves, very thinly sliced
- 10 basil leaves, finely chopped
- 2 tbsp finely chopped flat-leaf parsley, plus extra to serve
- 3 vine-ripened tomatoes, seeded, diced
- 1 tbsp salted baby capers, rinsed

PASTA DOUGH
- 700 gm (6⅓ cups) "00" flour
- 7 eggs

1 For pasta dough, place flour in a bowl and make a well in the centre. Crack eggs into the well and mix with a fork, then start incorporating flour into the eggs, using your hand to combine. Turn dough out onto a lightly floured bench and knead until smooth (10 minutes). You may need to add more flour if the dough is sticky. Wrap in plastic wrap and rest for 30 minutes. Roll a quarter of the dough through a pasta machine, starting on the widest setting and reducing a notch at a time, and rolling and folding and passing pasta through each setting a couple of times, until the second-to-last setting. Pass it through the spaghetti setting, then hang it over a wooden broom handle or clothes rack to dry in a draught-free room (1 hour). Repeat with remaining dough.

2 Kill lobsters humanely (see cook's notes p279), then remove the heads using a heavy knife. Boil lobsters in a large saucepan of heavily salted water for 4 minutes, then refresh in iced water. Remove all the meat from the shells (reserve shells and heads to make stock for another use), chop coarsely and refrigerate until required.

3 When ready to serve, bring a large saucepan of salted water to the boil. Heat butter and oil in a large saucepan over medium heat, add garlic and sauté until pale golden (2-3 minutes). Add lobster meat, basil, parsley, tomatoes and capers, season to taste and simmer until tomatoes have broken down (5 minutes). You may need to add extra olive oil for a smoother sauce. Keep warm.

4 Cook pasta in the boiling water until al dente (1-2 minutes). Drain, reserving 200ml cooking water, and toss pasta with the lobster mixture, adding enough reserved pasta water so the sauce coats pasta well. Serve hot.

WINE SUGGESTIONS A white Burgundy or other chardonnay.

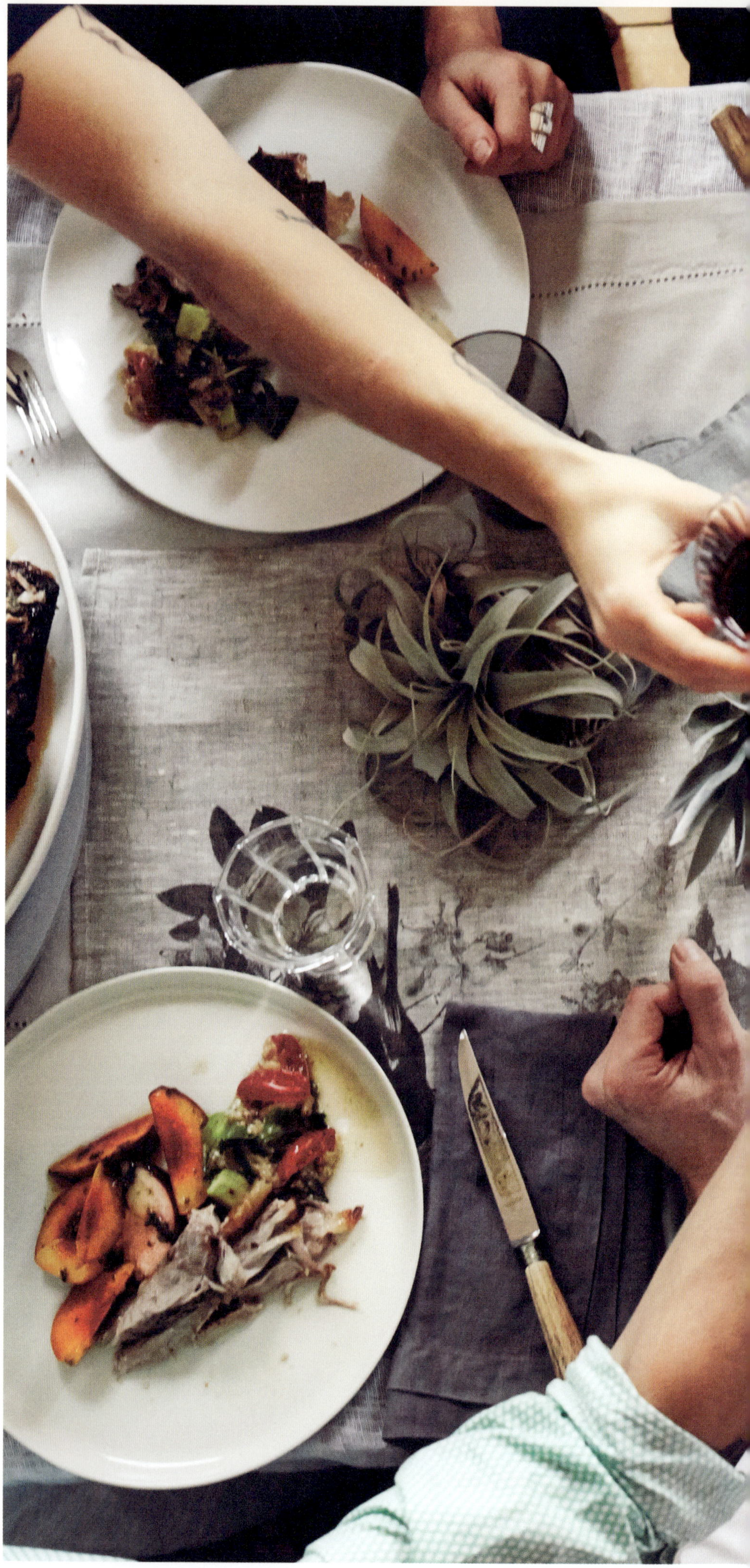

CHRISTMAS FEAST

CHRISTMAS FEAST

ROAST SHOULDER OF PORK

"I like to use a free-range old-breed pig such as Berkshire or large black," says Hafner. "They have a much better flavour and the fat is soft and delicious. They also seem to make the best crackling. I ask for a female pig – their flavour is better. Order one at your local farmers' market or specialist butcher. Leave the pork in the fridge uncovered overnight – it helps to dry the skin, which makes good crackling. I like to cook pork gently and past well done so it falls off the bone. This requires some attention. Take the pork out of the oven and give the meat a prod – when it's ready it will yield; if it springs back, return it to the oven for another 15 minutes. If you find that the crackling has not quite crackled enough, turn the heat up to 200C and give the pork one last blast – that should do it." Start this recipe a day ahead to dry the pork skin.

PREP TIME 15 MINS, COOK 4 HRS (PLUS DRYING)
SERVES 8-10

—

- 1 whole pork shoulder (4kg), bone in and skin scored (see note)
- 1 cup coarsely chopped wild fennel fronds (see note)
- Finely grated rind of 3 lemons
- 2 tbsp coarsely chopped rosemary
- 4 garlic cloves, finely chopped
- 1½ tbsp extra-virgin olive oil
- 6 celery stalks, coarsely chopped
- 3 carrots, coarsely chopped
- 3 onions, coarsely chopped
- 400 ml light red wine

1 Refrigerate scored pork uncovered overnight to dry out the skin. Remove from the fridge an hour before cooking.
2 Preheat oven to 190C. Pound fennel, lemon rind, rosemary and garlic to a paste with a mortar and pestle. Add oil, then rub marinade into the flesh of the pork (not the skin), season, cover with a tea towel and stand at room temperature for 45 minutes.
3 Scatter celery, carrot and onion in a large roasting pan and place pork on top. Rub the skin with 1 tbsp oil and sprinkle generously with fine sea salt (about 15gm; don't worry about the amount of salt – it helps the crackling form and you brush it off later). Reduce oven to 180C and roast pork for 1 hour, then add a third of the wine to the pan, reduce oven to 165C and continue to roast pork, topping up with wine (and water if needed) so there's always liquid in the bottom of the pan – this keeps pork juicy and makes a delicious sauce – until meat falls from the bone, and skin has crackled well (4kg pork will take about 4 hours). Set aside to rest for 30-40 minutes.
4 Transfer pork to a carving board – carefully lifting the pork wearing kitchen gloves works best – and brush off excess salt. Strain pan juices into a saucepan and skim off the fat, then taste – add a little water if it's too strong, or reduce it further to concentrate the flavours. Serve with pork.
NOTE Ask your butcher to score the pork skin for you. Wild fennel can be found growing along creeks and rivers, or use 2 tbsp fennel seeds, ground.
WINE SUGGESTIONS A great pinot noir such as a Chambertin from the Côte de Nuits, or, keeping it local, Bass Phillip Premium Pinot Noir, Cobaw Ridge, or a Sinapius pinot noir.

SMOKY EGGPLANT AND POMEGRANATE SALAD

"This salad is sweet, sour and smoky all at once, making for a good balance with the richness of the roast pork," says Hafner.

PREP TIME 15 MINS, COOK 10 MINS (PLUS STANDING)
SERVES 8-10

—

- 6 small eggplant (200gm each)
- 4 Lebanese cucumbers, seeds removed, coarsely diced
- 4 vine-ripened tomatoes, sliced into wedges
- 1 small red chilli, thinly sliced
- 2 tbsp pomegranate molasses
- Juice of 2 lemons
- 80 ml ($\frac{1}{3}$ cup) extra-virgin olive oil
- $\frac{3}{4}$ cup (loosely packed) coriander leaves
- $\frac{1}{2}$ cup (loosely packed) mint leaves, coarsely chopped
- 1 tbsp sumac

1 Cook eggplants over an open flame or medium-high grill, turning occasionally, until blackened all over (8-10 minutes). When cool enough to handle, halve lengthways and gently scoop out the flesh, being careful not to take the charred skin with it. Chop into large pieces and combine in a bowl with cucumber, tomato and chilli.

2 Combine pomegranate molasses, lemon juice and extra-virgin olive oil in a separate bowl, and pour onto eggplant mixture, then stand for 10 minutes for flavours to develop. Taste for seasoning – it should be sharp, sour and sweet – and adjust as necessary. Add herbs and sumac, toss to combine and serve.

NECTARINE SALAD

"This salad is best made just before serving," Hafner says.

PREP TIME 10 MINS (PLUS STANDING)
SERVES 8-10

—

- 60 ml ($\frac{1}{4}$ cup) extra-virgin olive oil
- Juice of 1-2 limes, to taste
- 2 tbsp light muscovado sugar
- 5 firm but ripe white or yellow nectarines, cut into thick wedges
- $\frac{1}{3}$ cup (firmly packed) mint, finely chopped

1 Combine extra-virgin olive oil, lime juice and muscovado sugar in a bowl, season to taste and adjust sweetness and acidity to balance. Stand for 5 minutes until sugar dissolves.

2 Add nectarines and mint, toss to combine and serve.

CHRISTMAS FEAST

CHRISTMAS FEAST

CHOCOLATE AND TURKISH COFFEE GRANITA WITH POACHED CHERRIES

"This beautiful and exotic sorbet comes from my time working with Greg Malouf," says Hafner. *"I've always loved it."* Chill the glasses before serving this dessert.

PREP TIME 35 MINS, COOK 10 MINS (PLUS FREEZING, COOLING)
MAKES 8-10

1	heaped tbsp finely ground Turkish coffee (see note)
375	gm caster sugar
150	gm liquid glucose
3	cardamom pods, bruised
100	gm Dutch-process cocoa
200	gm crème fraîche
100	ml pouring cream
2	tbsp caster sugar
1	tsp vanilla bean paste

POACHED CHERRIES

220	gm (1 cup) caster sugar
1	cinnamon quill
2	star anise
500	gm fresh cherries, pitted

1 Pour 80ml of boiling water over coffee in a bowl and leave to infuse for a few minutes, then strain into a saucepan through a muslin cloth or fine sieve. Add sugar, liquid glucose, cardamom pods, cocoa powder and 1.25 litres water, and gently bring to the boil, whisking until combined, and simmer for 5 minutes. Strain through a fine sieve into a cold bowl (discard solids) and set aside to cool (30 minutes). Pour into a container and freeze, scraping it with a fork every half an hour to create ice crystals, until it is completely frozen and fluffy (2-4 hours), then freeze until required. Fluff up the crystals again before serving.

2 For poached cherries, combine sugar and spices in a saucepan over high heat with 250ml water and bring to the boil, then reduce heat to low and simmer for 5 minutes. Add cherries, then place a round of baking paper directly on top and gently simmer until cherries are just tender (7 minutes). Set aside to cool in the syrup, then refrigerate until chilled.

3 Whisk crème fraîche, pouring cream, sugar and vanilla bean paste in a bowl until soft peaks form.

4 Spoon cherries into chilled glasses, top with cream and granita, and serve immediately.

NOTE Turkish coffee is available from Middle Eastern grocers.
DRINK SUGGESTION A fragrant grappa or a vintage Port.

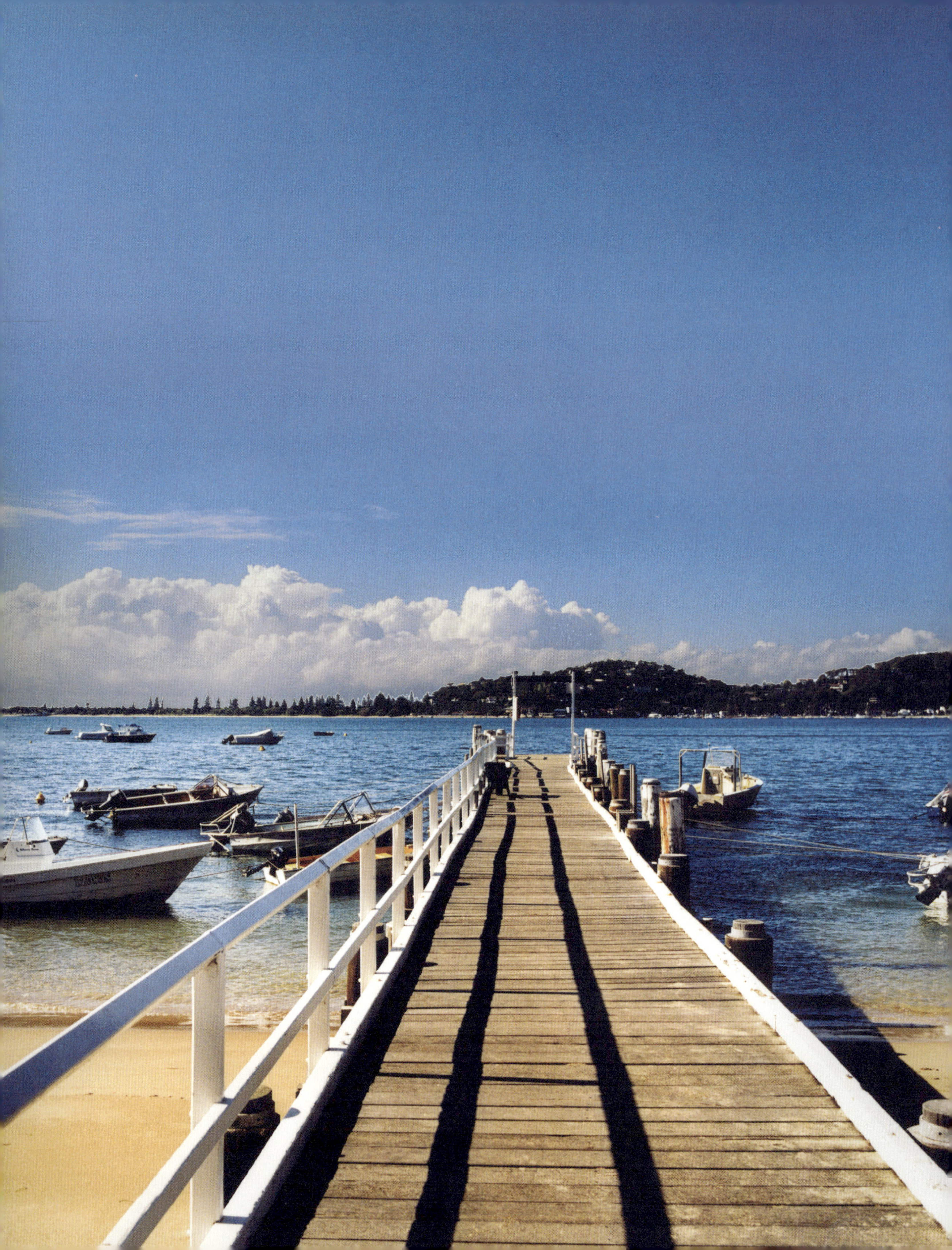

LUNCH BY THE BEACH

Whether you're entertaining deck-side, pool-side or beach-side, this is the perfect laid-back menu. Chill the drinks, light the barbecue and kick off your shoes – it's summer lunch at its most effortless.

—

+ Sparkling passionfruit cordial

+ Kingfish ceviche with young coconut and lime

+ Scallops with brown-bread butter and pancetta

+ Gin-cured ocean trout with herb crust

+ Potato and leek salad with mustard dressing

+ Grilled chicken with pickled watermelon salad

+ Golden pavlova with mango yoghurt and tropical fruits

—

SPARKLING PASSIONFRUIT CORDIAL

PREP TIME 20 MINS, COOK 10 MINS (PLUS COOLING)
SERVES 8

—

Ice cubes, lime wedges, mint sprigs and sparkling mineral water, to serve

PASSIONFRUIT CORDIAL

350 ml passionfruit pulp (from about 8 Panama passionfruit)
385 gm (1¾ cups) caster sugar
60 ml (¼ cup) lime juice
2 tsp white vinegar

1 For passionfruit cordial, process pulp in a food processor to separate juice from seeds, then strain through a sieve to yield 250ml liquid. Transfer to a large saucepan over medium-high heat, add sugar, lime juice and 150ml water and stir until sugar dissolves. Bring to the boil, reduce heat to medium and simmer until syrupy (6-8 minutes). Remove from heat, add vinegar, skim scum from surface, transfer to a sterile bottle and refrigerate until cool. Makes about 500ml. Passionfruit cordial will keep refrigerated for a month.

2 To serve, pour passionfruit cordial to taste into tall glasses filled with ice, squeeze in lime wedges, add mint, top up with mineral water, stir to combine and serve.

LUNCH BY THE BEACH

LUNCH BY THE BEACH

KINGFISH CEVICHE WITH YOUNG COCONUT AND LIME

Pulling this appetiser together is a snap. You can have everything prepped and ready to go, then all you need to do is combine the ingredients just before serving.

PREP TIME 20 MINS
SERVES 8

—

- 800 gm skinless kingfish fillet, diced
- 80 ml (⅓ cup) coconut milk
- Juice of 4 limes and finely grated rind of 2, plus extra finely grated rind to serve
- ¼ cup (loosely packed) coriander, coarsely chopped
- 1 Lebanese cucumber, half peeled, seeds removed, cut into small dice
- 1 pickled jalapeño, finely chopped
- Finely chopped young coconut, to serve

1 Combine kingfish, coconut milk, lime juice and rind, coriander, cucumber, and jalapeño in a bowl. Season to taste and stir to combine. Spoon into small chilled glasses, scatter with young coconut and extra lime rind and serve.

WINE SUGGESTION Citrusy young dry riesling.

SCALLOPS WITH BROWN-BREAD BUTTER AND PANCETTA

You can prepare the brown-bread butter ahead of time and have it on hand for when unexpected guests pop in. It works equally well on grilled fish.

PREP TIME 15 MINS, COOK 10 MINS (PLUS CHILLING)
SERVES 8

—

32	scallops on the half shell
150	gm mild flat pancetta, cut into lardons
	Baby herbs, cress, lemon wedges and crusty bread, to serve

BROWN-BREAD BUTTER

250	gm softened butter
80	gm fresh fine brown or rye breadcrumbs
$\frac{1}{2}$	cup (loosely packed) finely chopped mixed herbs, such as flat-leaf parsley, basil, thyme and dill
2	spring onions, finely chopped
1	garlic clove, finely chopped
	Finely grated rind of 1 lemon and juice of $\frac{1}{2}$

1 For brown-bread butter, beat butter in an electric mixer until light and fluffy (1-2 minutes). Add remaining ingredients and beat to just combine, then season to taste. Spoon butter along the length of a 30cm-long piece of plastic wrap, roll to form a long sausage, then pinch ends and roll to form a tight cylinder. Refrigerate until firm or until required (2-3 hours; brown-bread butter will keep refrigerated for a week).

2 Preheat grill to high heat. Place half the scallops on an oven tray lined with foil. Slice half the brown-bread butter into thin rounds, place on top of scallops, then top with pancetta and grill until scallops are cooked through and pancetta is crisp (3-5 minutes). Repeat with remaining scallops, butter and pancetta. Scatter with herbs and cress and serve warm with lemon wedges and crusty bread.

WINE SUGGESTION Crisp Italian white, such as a vermentino.

LUNCH BY THE BEACH

LUNCH BY THE BEACH

GIN-CURED OCEAN TROUT WITH HERB CRUST

Lightly curing the fish before roasting adds another dimension of flavour and texture. You can extend the curing time by up to a week and serve it in the same manner as gravlax. Begin this recipe at least a day ahead to cure the trout.

**PREP TIME 45 MINS, COOK TIME 10 MINS
(PLUS CURING, COOLING, CHILLING)
SERVES 6-8**

—

- 200 gm caster sugar
- 140 gm sea salt
- 120 ml gin
- 40 gm finely grated fresh horseradish (or shop-bought)
- 1 cup (loosely packed) dill, finely chopped
- 2 sides skinless ocean trout (1.2kg each), pin-bones removed
- 30 ml olive oil
- 2 tbsp each finely chopped mint, flat-leaf parsley and chervil
- Finely grated rind of 2 lemons
- Lemon wedges, to serve

CUCUMBER PICKLE
- 2 tsp fennel seeds
- 160 ml white wine vinegar
- 80 ml dry white wine
- 60 gm caster sugar
- 2 Lebanese cucumbers, thinly sliced on a mandolin
- 2 golden shallots, thinly sliced

1 Combine sugar, salt, gin, horseradish and dill, reserving 2 tbsp dill to serve, in a bowl with plenty of freshly ground black pepper. Spread half the curing mixture in base of a non-reactive dish (see cook's notes p279) and place trout on top. Spread remaining mixture on top of trout, cover with plastic wrap and refrigerate overnight to cure.

2 Meanwhile, for cucumber pickle, dry-roast fennel seeds until fragrant (1 minute; see cook's notes p279), then crush using a mortar and pestle and return to pan. Add vinegar, wine, sugar and 100ml water, season to taste and bring to the boil, then cool to room temperature. Combine cucumber and shallot in a non-reactive container, pour in pickling liquid in and refrigerate until chilled and lightly pickled (1-1½ hours).

3 Preheat oven to 200C. Brush curing mixture from trout and pat dry with paper towels. Place in a roasting pan lined with baking paper and drizzle with oil. Roast until just golden and cooked to your liking (4-6 minutes for medium-rare).

4 Meanwhile, combine mint, parsley, chervil, lemon rind and reserved dill in a bowl and season to taste. Scatter mixture over trout and serve warm with cucumber pickle and lemon wedges.

WINE SUGGESTIONS Sparkling rosé or Champagne.

POTATO AND LEEK SALAD
WITH MUSTARD DRESSING
(TOP LEFT)

POTATO AND LEEK SALAD WITH MUSTARD DRESSING

PREP TIME 25 MINS, COOK 20 MINS (PLUS COOLING)
SERVES 8

—

- 1.6 kg small sebago potatoes, scrubbed
- 100 ml extra-virgin olive oil
- 1 leek, halved lengthways and thinly sliced
- 2 garlic cloves, finely chopped
- 150 gm crème fraîche
- Finely grated rind and juice of 2 lemons, or to taste
- 2 tbsp Dijon mustard
- 1½ cups (loosely packed) wild rocket, trimmed

1 Cover potatoes in a large saucepan with plenty of cold salted water, bring to a simmer and cook until tender when pierced with a skewer (10-15 minutes). Drain and, when cool enough to handle, cut potatoes into thick wedges.

2 Meanwhile, heat half the oil in a frying pan over medium-high heat, add leek and garlic and sauté until softened and light golden (5-6 minutes). Transfer to a bowl and cool to room temperature. Add crème fraîche, lemon rind and juice, mustard and remaining oil, whisk until combined and season to taste.

3 Add dressing to potatoes, toss to coat, then add rocket, toss lightly to combine and serve.

WINE SUGGESTION Vibrant young sauvignon blanc.

LUNCH BY THE BEACH

GRILLED CHICKEN WITH PICKLED WATERMELON SALAD

Begin this recipe a day ahead to pickle the watermelon.

**PREP TIME 25 MINS, COOK 1 HR 20 MINS
(PLUS COOLING, PICKLING, MARINATING, RESTING)
SERVES 8**

—

- 2 chickens (about 1.8kg each), butterflied, backbone removed
- 160 gm light palm sugar, crushed
- 250 ml (1 cup) fish sauce
- 250 ml (1 cup) lime juice
- 150 gm (1 cup) spelt (see note)
- 600 gm watermelon, thickly sliced (reserve rind for pickle)
- 2 cups (loosely packed) mint
- 1 cup each (loosely packed) coriander, Thai basil and Vietnamese mint, plus extra to serve

PICKLED WATERMELON RIND
- 100 gm watermelon rind, thinly sliced on a mandolin
- 250 ml (1 cup) rice wine vinegar
- 165 gm (¾ cup) caster sugar
- 1 long red chilli, split
- 5 gm (1cm piece) ginger, thinly sliced

CRISP SHALLOTS AND GARLIC
- Vegetable oil, for deep-frying
- 10 golden shallots, thinly sliced on a mandolin
- 5 garlic cloves, thinly sliced on a mandolin

1 For pickled watermelon rind, place rind in a non-reactive container (see cook's notes p279) and set aside. Stir vinegar and sugar in a small saucepan over medium heat until sugar dissolves, bring to the boil, then set aside to cool. When cool, add chilli and ginger, and pour mixture over watermelon rind. Cover and refrigerate overnight to pickle.

2 Place chickens in a non-reactive dish and set aside. Pound palm sugar, fish sauce and lime juice using a large mortar and pestle, then pour half the mixture over chickens and refrigerate, turning occasionally, for 1 hour to marinate. Refrigerate remaining dressing until required.

3 Meanwhile, cook spelt in boiling water until tender (30-40 minutes). Drain well, spread on a tray and set aside to cool.

4 For crisp shallots and garlic, heat vegetable oil in a deep saucepan to 160C, add shallot and deep-fry in batches, stirring frequently, until crisp and golden (1-2 minutes; be careful, hot oil will spit). Remove with a slotted spoon and drain on paper towels. Repeat with garlic. Store separately in airtight containers until required.

5 Heat a char-grill pan over medium-high heat (or use a barbecue). Drain chickens from marinade and grill skin-side down until crisp (10-15 minutes), then turn and grill until cooked through (10-15 minutes). Set aside to rest for 10-15 minutes.

6 Combine watermelon wedges, spelt, herbs and pickled watermelon rind in a bowl, drizzle with reserved dressing and toss to combine. Scatter chicken with crisp shallots and garlic, and extra herbs, and serve with pickled watermelon salad.

NOTE Spelt, a grain, similar to barley, is available from health-food shops and select delicatessens. If it's unavailable, substitute freekah or farro perlato.

WINE SUGGESTION Full-flavoured rosé made from grenache.

LUNCH BY THE BEACH

LUNCH BY THE BEACH

GOLDEN PAVLOVA WITH MANGO YOGHURT AND TROPICAL FRUITS

The mango yoghurt and rum and lime caramel can be made a few days ahead to make things easier, but the pavlova itself is best made on the day. Begin this recipe a day ahead to drain the yoghurt.

PREP TIME 40 MINS, COOK 2 HRS 10 MINS (PLUS DRAINING, CHILLING, COOLING)
SERVES 8

- 6 eggwhites
- ¼ tsp cream of tartar
- 250 gm raw caster sugar
- 40 gm brown sugar
- Scraped seeds of 1 vanilla bean
- 35 gm (¼ cup) cornflour
- 3 tsp white vinegar
- 3 bananas, thickly sliced
- 2 mangoes, thickly sliced
- 500 gm (about ½) pineapple, thinly sliced
- Pulp of 2 passionfruit
- Mint, to serve

MANGO YOGHURT
- 1 kg Greek-style yoghurt
- 250 gm mango (about 1), coarsely chopped
- 80 gm raw caster sugar
- Juice of 1 lime
- 300 gm sour cream

RUM AND LIME CARAMEL
- 330 gm (1½ cups) raw caster sugar
- 70 ml golden rum
- 60 ml (¼ cup) lime juice
- ½ cup (firmly packed) mint

1 For mango yoghurt, place yoghurt in a sieve lined with muslin over a bowl and refrigerate overnight to drain. Process mango, sugar and lime juice in a food processor until smooth. Transfer to a saucepan and bring to a simmer, then cook, stirring occasionally, until syrupy (2-3 minutes). Cool, then refrigerate until chilled. Whisk yoghurt and sour cream together in a bowl, fold in mango mixture and refrigerate until required.

2 Preheat oven to 120C. Whisk eggwhites, cream of tartar and a pinch of salt in an electric mixer until firm peaks form (4-5 minutes). Whisking continuously, add sugars 1 tbsp at a time until mixture is stiff and glossy (4-5 minutes), then whisk in vanilla seeds and fold in cornflour and vinegar. Form mixture into a 20cm-diameter circle on an oven tray lined with baking paper, bake until crisp and dry (1½-2 hours), then turn off oven and cool completely with door ajar.

3 Meanwhile, for rum and lime caramel, stir sugar and 180ml water in a saucepan over medium-high heat until sugar dissolves, then bring to the boil and cook until dark caramel (5-6 minutes). Remove from heat and add 100ml water (be careful, hot caramel will spit), rum, lime juice and mint and cool to room temperature. Strain (discard mint) and refrigerate until required. Rum and lime caramel will keep refrigerated for a week.

4 Top pavlova with mango yoghurt, then pile fruit on top, drizzle with a little rum and lime caramel, scatter with mint and serve with remaining caramel on the side.

WINE SUGGESTION Pink moscato.

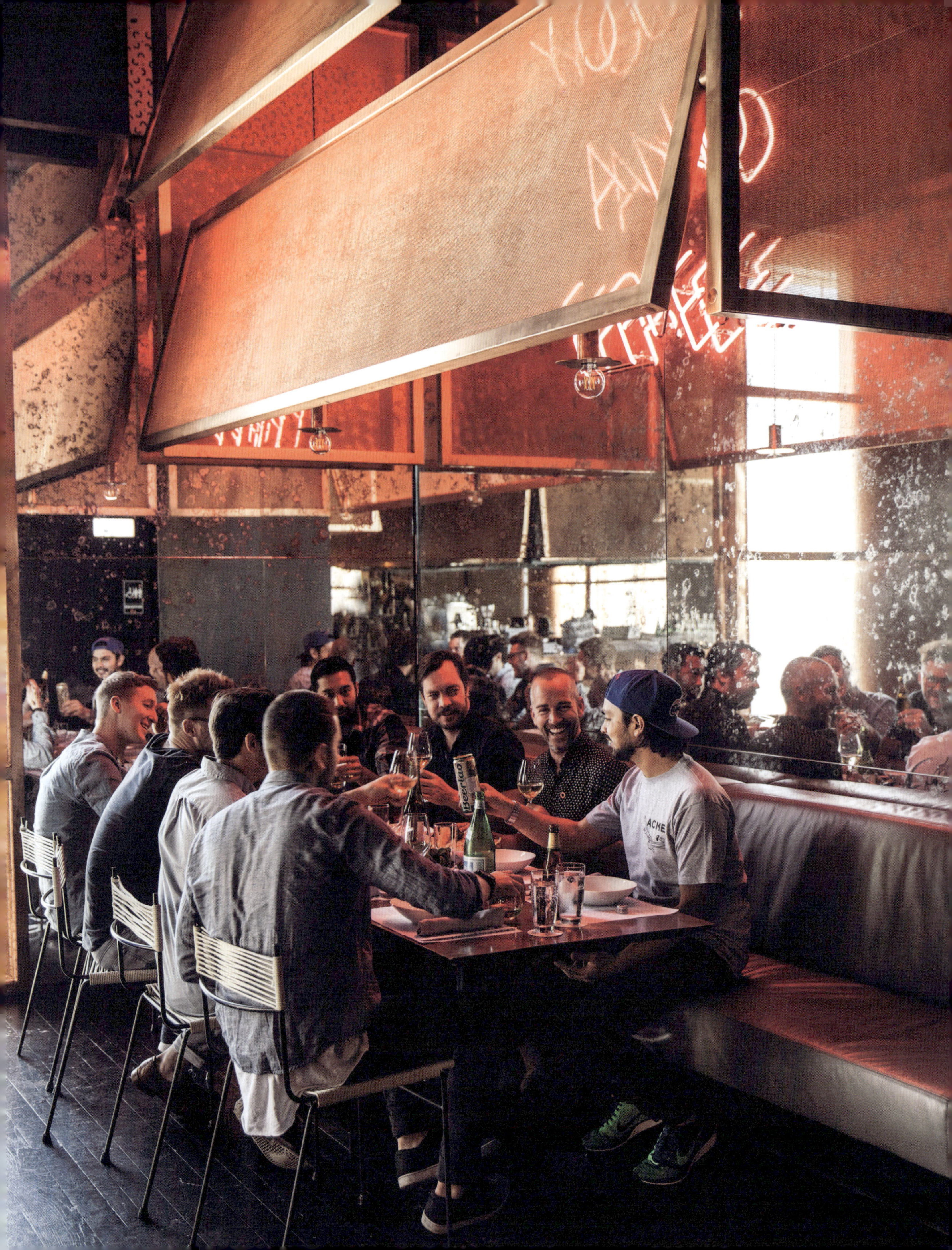

HOLLYWOOD DINNER PARTY

If your idea of a dinner party extends to nachos and flash-fried chicken, then this menu from the Aussie team behind Los Angeles hotspot EP & LP is just what you're looking for. Crank up the tunes and get it while it's hot.

—

+ LP nachos

+ Nama sea pearls

+ Turmeric and coconut salmon curry

+ Egg and vegetable fried rice

+ Wood-fired rib-eye with jaew, butter lettuce and Asian herbs

+ Loudogg's twice-cooked crisp-skinned chicken

+ Affogato "my style"

—

HOLLYWOOD DINNER PARTY

LP NACHOS

NAMA SEA PEARLS

LP NACHOS

"This is my version of a traditional Thai dish called lon, but I call it nachos," says chef Louis Tikaram. *"It's still served with raw cucumber and cabbage, but I've also incorporated cassava crackers for crunch, and with nachos people know exactly what to do. I use pork in this recipe, although you could substitute chicken or even add chopped prawns if you like. Either way, it must be eaten with a cold beer."*

PREP TIME 30 MINS, COOK 40 MINS
SERVES 6-8

Vegetable oil, for deep-frying
150 gm cassava crackers (see note)
20 gm ginger, coarsely chopped
2 garlic cloves, coarsely chopped
2 tbsp coconut oil
500 gm coarsely minced pork neck
1 litre (4 cups) coconut cream
500 ml (2 cups) chicken stock
60 ml (¼ cup) Thai yellow soy bean paste (see note)
60 ml (¼ cup) fish sauce
50 gm (2 tbsp) tamarind paste (see note)
1 tbsp grated soft palm sugar
Pinch of roasted chilli powder or chilli flakes
Thinly sliced lemongrass, long red chilli, red shallot, kaffir lime leaves, coriander and lime wedges, to serve
2 Lebanese cucumbers, thickly sliced diagonally

1 Heat oil in a wok or deep saucepan to 180C and deep-fry cassava crackers, two or three at a time, turning once, until puffed, golden and crisp (20-30 seconds). Drain on paper towels and cool to room temperature.

2 Pound ginger and garlic with a mortar and pestle to a fine paste (1-2 minutes). Heat coconut oil in a saucepan or large wok over high heat, add ginger-garlic paste and stir-fry until golden brown and fragrant (30-40 seconds). Add pork and stir-fry until browned (2-3 minutes), breaking up any clumps, then add coconut cream, stock and soy bean paste and simmer until liquid is almost reduced (25-30 minutes). Season to taste with fish sauce, tamarind, palm sugar and chilli powder – the lon should taste salty, sour, slightly sweet and creamy. Scatter with lemongrass, chilli, shallot and kaffir lime leaves, and serve hot with coriander, lime wedges and cucumber.

NOTE Cassava crackers, Thai yellow soy bean paste and tamarind paste are all available from Asian grocers.

DRINK SUGGESTION A light Mexican or Asian beer, such as Corona, Asahi or Singha.

NAMA SEA PEARLS

"This is a traditional Fijian seaweed dish served as part of a shared meal, although it's delicious by itself as a starter or snack," says Tikaram. "In Los Angeles, I use a Hawaiian seaweed similar to what I used in Fiji. For all you Aussies, there's now a Fijian family company called Pacific Seaweeds that sells nama just as I used to buy it from Suva Market on Saturday mornings."

PREP TIME 30 MINS
SERVES 6-8

—

2 mature coconuts
200 gm nama sea pearls (see note)
2 Roma tomatoes, quartered, seeded, finely chopped
2 red shallots, finely chopped
2 long red chillies, halved, seeded, thinly sliced
Juice of $1\frac{1}{2}$ limes or to taste
Micro-coriander and quartered cherry tomatoes, to serve

1 Crack open coconuts with the back of a heavy knife or cleaver over a bowl (reserve water to use in curries or soups; it keeps refrigerated for 1-2 days), scrape out the white flesh with a coconut scraper (see note), stopping at the brown membrane. Mix flesh in a large bowl with 125ml cold water then, working in batches, squeeze through a piece of cheesecloth to extract as much milk as possible. Makes about 350ml.

2 Rinse nama in a sieve under slow-running cold water until bright and plump (20 seconds; be brief so as not to rinse off all the sea flavour). Drain well, then combine in a large bowl with coconut milk, tomato, shallot, chilli and a pinch of salt. Squeeze in lime juice to taste and serve in small bowls or, as served at the restaurant, in the coconut shells. The flavour should be hot and rich from the chilli and fresh coconut milk, and the nama will burst in the mouth with sea-like salty flavour. Serve scattered with micro-coriander and cherry tomatoes.

NOTE Coconut scrapers are available from Asian supermarkets, but you can also remove the flesh from the shell, peel off the skin and grate it finely. Nama sea pearls or sea grapes are a sea succulent. Also known as umibudo, they're available from Good Grub Hub (goodgrubhub.com).

WINE SUGGESTION Champagne.

70 GOURMET TRAVELLER | MENUS

FROM LEFT:
DAVID COMBES,
LOUIS TIKARAM
& GRANT SMILLIE

HOLLYWOOD DINNER PARTY

TURMERIC AND COCONUT SALMON CURRY

"This light aromatic coconut-based curry from Thailand is a great way to showcase beautiful fresh seafood," says Tikaram. "I use salmon here, although you could substitute mussels, squid or a combination of them all. At EP we make all our curry pastes fresh daily. It's expensive and labour-intensive, but the result is delicious; I must admit, though, that when I make a quick curry at home, I use a store-bought yellow curry paste, which does the job."

PREP TIME 45 MINS, COOK 15 MINS (PLUS SOAKING)
SERVES 6-8

- 1 litre (4 cups) chicken stock
- 250 ml (1 cup) coconut cream
- ¼ cup (about 12) kaffir lime leaves
- 2 lemongrass stalks, cut into 3-4 sections
- 1 tbsp tamarind paste or concentrate mixed with 1 tbsp water
- 2 tbsp fish sauce
- 2 tbsp oyster sauce
- 1 tbsp white sugar
- 500 gm skinless boneless salmon fillet
- 100 gm (½ bunch) snake beans, cut into rough 6cm lengths
- 2 long red chillies, seeded and cut into julienne
- ½ cup (loosely packed) Thai basil, plus extra to serve
- Juice of 2 mandarins
- Thai basil, thinly sliced kaffir lime leaf and steamed jasmine rice, to serve

YELLOW CURRY PASTE
- 12 dried long red chillies
- 20 gm galangal, thinly sliced
- 1½ tbsp thinly sliced lemongrass (pale tender part only)
- 10 gm fresh turmeric, thinly sliced
- 3 garlic cloves, peeled
- 3 tsp sliced krachai (see note)
- ½ tsp shrimp paste (see note)

1 For yellow curry paste, soak chillies in a bowl of warm water for 20 minutes, then drain, reserving soaking water, and process in a small blender or food processor with remaining ingredients until smooth, adding a little water to help blend if necessary. Refrigerate until required.

2 Bring stock, coconut cream, kaffir lime leaves and lemongrass to the boil in a saucepan over medium heat, add 4 tbsp curry paste (refrigerate any remaining in an airtight container for up to a week) and simmer until aromatic and mixture no longer tastes raw (3-5 minutes). Add tamarind, fish sauce, oyster sauce and sugar, then add salmon and simmer very gently over low heat until almost cooked (5-6 minutes). Add snake beans, chilli and basil, and simmer until salmon is just cooked (1-2 minutes). Stir in mandarin juice, adjust seasoning if necessary and serve hot with extra Thai basil, kaffir lime leaf and rice.

NOTE Krachai, or wild ginger, is available fresh from Thai grocers when in season, or in jars from Asian greengrocers. Shrimp paste, also called kapi or terasi, is available from Asian food stores.

DRINK SUGGESTIONS A fruity beer like Stone & Wood Pacific Ale, or a high-acidity white wine like chenin blanc or sauvignon blanc.

EGG AND VEGETABLE
FRIED RICE (TOP)

HOLLYWOOD DINNER PARTY

HOLLYWOOD DINNER PARTY

EGG AND VEGETABLE FRIED RICE

"This is an awesome dish for using up leftover rice," says Tikaram. "It was a staple in my home when I was growing up, as a snack after basketball practice. My secret to good fried rice is using four types of sauce to season it – if you want to make it vegetarian, leave out the fish sauce and oyster sauce."

PREP TIME 15 MINS, COOK 5 MINS
SERVES 6-8

- 80 ml (⅓ cup) canola oil
- 2 eggs
- 260 gm snake beans, thinly sliced
- 200 gm baby corn, thinly sliced
- 1 kg (8 cups) cooked white or brown jasmine rice (see note)
- 2 tsp fish sauce
- 2 tsp soy sauce
- 2 tsp oyster sauce
- 2 tsp sweet soy sauce
- 1 handful bean sprouts
- 1 Lebanese cucumber, sliced diagonally
- 1 lime, cut into wedges

1 Heat oil in a large wok over high heat until smoking hot, then crack in eggs and stir-fry so they break up and cook evenly (1 minute). Add vegetables, stir-fry for 30 seconds, then add rice and stir, toss and squish with your spoon to separate the grains; adjust heat while you cook so rice doesn't burn. Season with sauces and salt to taste and continue to toss and stir-fry until rice is completely separated and the aroma of toasted rice fills the room (3-4 minutes). Serve with bean sprouts, cucumber and lime wedges.

NOTE For 1kg cooked rice, bring 600gm (3 cups) jasmine rice and 3 cups water to the boil in a covered saucepan over high heat, then reduce heat to low and simmer for 10 minutes. Remove from heat and transfer rice to a bowl to cool. If you're making fried rice the same day, transfer rice to trays lined with baking paper and refrigerate to chill for 2-3 hours before frying.

WOOD-FIRED RIB-EYE WITH JAEW,
BUTTER LETTUCE AND ASIAN HERBS

LOUDOGG'S TWICE-COOKED
CRISP-SKINNED CHICKEN

HOLLYWOOD DINNER PARTY

WOOD-FIRED RIB-EYE WITH JAEW, BUTTER LETTUCE AND ASIAN HERBS

"I am a huge fan of cooking over hardwood and charcoal so a wood grill is essential in my kitchen as is the barbecue at home," says Tikaram. "In this recipe, I'm cooking one of my favourite cuts – a dry-aged rib-eye steak with the bone in. The meat is flavoursome and tender, although you can cook whatever cut of beef you like. Jaew is a Thai dipping sauce, which is always on the table at any good Thai restaurant and in the homes of Thai families. The main ingredient of this jaew is dried chilli so it's hot, although teamed with the beautiful beef, lettuce and herbs, it's the perfect heat and complements the whole meal."

PREP TIME 20 MINS, COOK 20 MINS (PLUS FIRE PREPARATION, RESTING)
SERVES 6-8

—

600 gm	dry-aged rib-eye steak, bone in, brought to room temperature
1 tsp	vegetable oil
1	butter lettuce, leaves separated and washed
½ cup each	(loosely packed) Vietnamese mint, coriander and Thai basil
	Lime wedges and steamed jasmine or sticky rice, to serve

JAEW

10 gm	(¼ cup) dried small Thai chillies
125 ml	(½ cup) lime juice
60 ml	(¼ cup) fish sauce
1 tsp	white sugar
1	spring onion, thinly sliced
2 tbsp	finely chopped coriander

1 Light a wood-fired barbecue and let it burn down to ensure you have a nice even heat by the time you are ready to cook (1-1½ hours).

2 For jaew, dry-roast chillies in a wok or frying pan over low heat until aromatic and roasted (2-3 minutes; this gives the jaew a beautiful smoky flavour, but be careful not to burn the chillies or they'll turn bitter). Cool, then pound with a mortar and pestle or slightly crush in a spice grinder until crunchy (not to a fine powder). Combine 3 tsp crushed roasted chilli in a small bowl with remaining ingredients and mix well. You may need to balance the flavour with more fish sauce or sugar; jaew should taste hot, sour, salty and slightly sweet. Refrigerate until required.

3 Lightly oil steak on both sides and season to taste with sea salt. Grill, turning once, until browned and cooked to your liking (5-7 minutes each side for medium-rare), then rest for 20 minutes. Cut beef off the bone, then slice across the grain and arrange on a serving plate. Serve with lettuce leaves, herbs, lime wedges, rice and jaew.

WINE SUGGESTION A big red will go with this dish, though Tikaram prefers a light pinot noir.

LOUDOGG'S TWICE-COOKED CRISP-SKINNED CHICKEN

"This dish has followed me halfway around the world," says Tikaram. "Even before the doors swung open at EP we were receiving emails asking if my crisp-skinned chicken would make it onto the summer opening menu. It's actually my guilty pleasure after a pumping Saturday night service to plate up a couple of these and have a beer with the chefs in the kitchen once we finish, so how could I say no? To make the dipping sauce, you'll need a mortar and pestle, and a lot of elbow grease to pound it out, but it's worth it. This recipe will make more than enough, so store it in an airtight container and enjoy it on everything."

PREP TIME 45 MINS, COOK 50 MINS (PLUS CHILLING, RESTING)
SERVES 6-8

—

- 2.5 litres (10 cups) chicken stock
- 125 ml ($\frac{1}{2}$ cup) light soy sauce
- 40 gm ginger, coarsely chopped
- 6 spring onions, coarsely chopped
- 2 tsp crushed white peppercorns
- 1 chicken (about 1.6kg)
- 2 litres canola oil, for deep-frying
- Lemon wedges, to serve

CHILLI-VINEGAR DIPPING SAUCE

- 160 ml ($\frac{2}{3}$ cup) canola oil
- 30 gm ($\frac{2}{3}$ cup) long dried red chillies, seeded
- 10 gm ginger, cut into julienne, plus extra to serve
- 25 gm ($\frac{1}{3}$ cup) fried shallots
- 25 gm ($\frac{1}{4}$ cup) fried garlic
- 1$\frac{1}{2}$ tsp white sugar
- 65 ml Chinkiang vinegar
- 70 ml light soy sauce
- Thinly sliced spring onion, to serve

1 Bring stock, soy sauce, ginger, spring onion and peppercorns to the boil in a deep saucepan slightly larger than the chicken in diameter. Submerge chicken completely, breast-side up, bring back to the boil, reduce heat to low and simmer for 20 minutes. Remove chicken with long tongs, drain well over saucepan, place on a plate breast-side up and stand for 30 minutes, then refrigerate until required. Cover with plastic wrap once cooled.

2 For chilli-vinegar dipping sauce, heat oil in a wok or deep frying pan to 160C. Flash-fry chillies, stirring continuously with a slotted spoon, until crisp and bright red (20 seconds). Remove with a slotted spoon and drain on paper towels. Add ginger and stir-fry until crisp and beginning to turn golden brown (40 seconds; stir frequently so ginger doesn't stick together). Remove with a slotted spoon and drain on paper towels. Strain oil into a saucepan or metal container and set aside to cool. Pound fried chillies and ginger, shallot, garlic and sugar with a large mortar and pestle until smooth (3-4 minutes). Add vinegar, soy sauce and 60ml reserved oil, and pound to a thick paste (1-2 minutes). Store in an airtight container in the refrigerator until required. Makes about 250ml. Chilli-vinegar dipping sauce will keep refrigerated for up to a week. Top with julienne ginger and spring onion before serving.

3 Bring chicken to room temperature and heat oil to 220C in a wok or large saucepan (if you have an electric deep-fryer, even better). Cut the chicken in half down the backbone with a large knife or cleaver, then carefully lower one half into the oil with tongs (be careful, hot oil will spit). Deep-fry, turning occasionally, until crisp, golden brown and cooked through (8-10 minutes), then drain on paper towels. Bring oil back to 220C and repeat with remaining chicken half, then season both to taste. Cut wings and legs off with a cleaver, cut each leg in two through the joint and each breast into three pieces through the bone. Arrange on a serving platter and serve hot with lemon wedges and chilli-vinegar dipping sauce.

DRINK SUGGESTIONS A pinot gris such as Holly's Garden or a full-body beer like Murray's Whale Ale.

HOLLYWOOD DINNER PARTY

AFFOGATO "MY STYLE"

"This is one of my favourite desserts to make at home – it's my take on the classic Italian affogato, although with some Fijian flair," says Tikaram. "If you don't have an ice-cream machine, use coconut sorbet from your local gelateria. A shot of any dark rum rounds it all out or you could leave it out, though if you ask my friends, it has to be Bounty."

PREP TIME 30 MINS, COOK 5 MINS (PLUS FREEZING)
SERVES 8

---

160 ml espresso
Bounty dark rum, to serve

COCONUT SORBET
180 gm caster sugar
250 gm liquid glucose
500 ml (2 cups) coconut cream
250 ml (1 cup) young coconut water (from about 1 young coconut)

1 For the sorbet, bring caster sugar and 180ml water to the boil in a small saucepan. Adjust heat to low and simmer to reduce slightly (2-3 minutes), then stir in glucose and set aside to cool completely (20-30 minutes). Add coconut cream, coconut water and a pinch of salt, whisk to combine, then churn in ice-cream machine. Freeze until required. Makes about 1 litre.

2 Scoop coconut sorbet into chilled glasses (you can do this an hour or so ahead of serving, then store them in the freezer), pour espresso and rum shots over sorbet, and serve immediately.

DRINK SUGGESTION More rum.

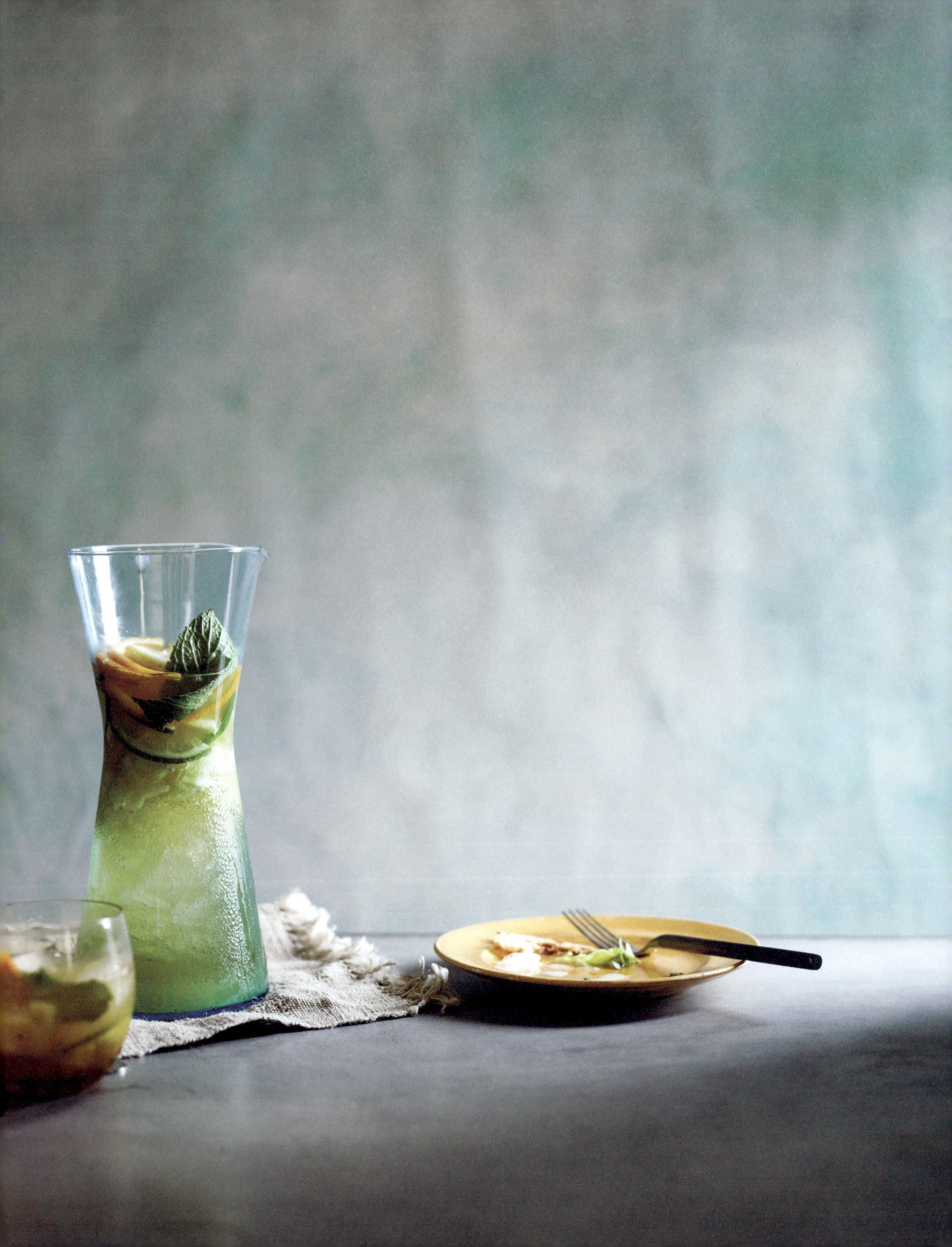

SMART-CASUAL LUNCH

Summer entertaining calls for a light, bright, breezy menu that's designed to impress with minimum fuss. Kick off with tropical cocktails and finish up with muscat-poached apricots. Lunch is served stat.

—

+ Pineapple, Mint, Ginger and Lime Crush

+ Crab and celery mayonnaise on crostini

+ Swordfish with agrodolce sauce

+ Roast beef and buttermilk

+ Asparagus with caper and shallot butter

+ Tomato and bread salad

+ Apricots poached in orange muscat with mascarpone and almonds

—

PINEAPPLE, MINT, GINGER
AND LIME CRUSH

CRAB AND CELERY MAYONNAISE
ON CROSTINI

84 GOURMET TRAVELLER | MENUS

SMART-CASUAL LUNCH

PINEAPPLE, MINT, GINGER AND LIME CRUSH

With its bright flavours, this punch is a great way to start any summer lunch. You can also make a batch without the gin for non-drinkers or designated drivers – they'll thank you for it. We like to use a good cloudy ginger beer with plenty of gingery kick.

PREP TIME 15 MINS, COOK 5 MINS
SERVES 6-8

- 400 gm coarsely chopped pineapple (about ½ pineapple)
- Juice of 3 limes and 2 oranges
- 50 gm finely grated ginger
- 180 ml gin
- Ginger beer, to taste
- Lemon, lime and orange slices and mint, to serve

VANILLA-MINT SYRUP
- 165 gm caster sugar
- 1 vanilla bean, split and seeds scraped
- ½ cup (firmly packed) mint

1 For vanilla-mint syrup, stir sugar and 125ml water in a saucepan over medium-high heat until sugar dissolves, then add vanilla bean and seeds, bring to the boil and cook until a light syrup forms (1-2 minutes). Remove from heat, add mint, pour into a container and refrigerate until chilled. Strain (discard mint and return vanilla pod to syrup), then refrigerate until required. This syrup keeps refrigerated for up to a month.

2 Pulse pineapple in a food processor to finely chop, then transfer to a jug, and add citrus juices, ginger and vanilla-mint syrup to taste. Add gin and plenty of ice, stir to chill, top up with ginger beer and serve garnished with citrus slices and mint.

CRAB AND CELERY MAYONNAISE ON CROSTINI

Crostini are ideal for fast entertaining: thin slices of bread quickly turned into serving vehicles for tasty toppings – anything from raw fish to smashed broad beans and pecorino.

PREP TIME 15, COOK 10 MINS
SERVES 6-8

—

- 1 celery heart, shaved on a mandolin, leaves reserved
- 2 tbsp extra-virgin olive oil
- 2 tsp white wine vinegar
- Large pinch of caster sugar
- 260 gm cooked spanner crab meat, drained
- 120 gm mayonnaise
- 2 tbsp basil cress, plus extra to serve
- 2 tbsp coarsely chopped chervil
- Tabasco, to taste
- 1 golden shallot, shaved lengthways into thin strips on a mandolin

CROSTINI
- 16 thin slices sourdough ciabatta
- Extra-virgin olive oil, for brushing
- 2 garlic cloves, halved

1 For crostini, preheat oven to 200C, brush ciabatta slices with oil and bake, turning once, until just golden (5-8 minutes). Rub with cut side of garlic and set aside.

2 For crab and celery mayonnaise, combine celery, oil, vinegar, sugar and a large pinch of salt in a bowl and set aside. Just before serving, toss in the crab, mayonnaise and herbs, season to taste with salt, pepper and Tabasco, and mix well.

3 Spoon crab mixture onto crostini, and serve scattered with extra basil cress and golden shallot.

WINE SUGGESTION Crisp dry riesling.

SMART-CASUAL LUNCH

SWORDFISH WITH AGRODOLCE SAUCE

Swordfish is great for entertaining – sear it just rare and then warm it in the oven to serve. The agrodolce sauce can be prepared a day ahead if you have the chance; simply toss the pine nuts, lemons and dill in at the last minute.

PREP TIME 15 MINS, COOK 10 MINS
SERVES 6-8

6-8	skinless swordfish steaks (250gm each)
	Olive oil, for brushing
	Lemon wedges, to serve

AGRODOLCE SAUCE

180	ml white wine vinegar
50	gm raw sugar
1½	Spanish onions, finely chopped
50	gm currants
60	gm pine nuts
2	lemons, segmented
½	cup dill sprigs

1 Preheat oven to 170C. For agrodolce sauce, bring vinegar and sugar to a simmer in a small saucepan over medium heat, stirring to dissolve sugar. Place onion in a bowl, pour vinegar mixture over, add currants and set aside for 5 minutes to steep. Meanwhile, roast pine nuts on an oven tray, shaking pan occasionally, until golden (4-6 minutes). Add to onion mixture along with lemon segments and set aside until ready to serve. Stir in the dill just before serving.

2 Heat a barbecue or char-grill pan over high heat. Brush swordfish steaks with olive oil and season to taste, then grill, in batches if necessary, turning once, until golden and cooked medium-rare (1½-2 minutes each side, depending on the thickness of the fish). Serve warm with agrodolce sauce spooned over and lemon wedges to the side.

WINE SUGGESTION Full-flavoured fiano.

ROAST BEEF WITH BUTTERMILK

Love-me-tender beef fillet is the perfect cut for quick cooking. Here we've seared it and kept it rare. It benefits from a good rest, so it's a great one to do ahead of time. For the best results, serve it at room temperature rather than cold from the fridge. A tangy buttermilk dressing and crunchy sprouts are all the adornment needed.

PREP TIME 10 MINS, COOK 12 MINS (PLUS RESTING)
SERVES 6-8

- 50 ml olive oil
- 2 pieces of mid-cut beef tenderloin (600gm each), at room temperature
- Mustard cress and crunchy sprouts, to serve

BUTTERMILK DRESSING
- 150 ml buttermilk
- 2 tbsp extra-virgin olive oil
- 1 tbsp sherry vinegar
- Finely grated rind and juice of ½ lemon, or to taste

1 Preheat oven to 220C. Heat oil in a large frying pan over high heat. Season beef all over, place in pan and brown all over (3-4 minutes). Transfer to oven and roast until cooked to your liking (6-8 minutes for medium-rare), then set aside at room temperature to rest for at least 10 minutes.
2 For buttermilk dressing, shake ingredients in a jar just before serving and season to taste.
3 To serve, thinly slice the beef across the grain and arrange on a platter, drizzle with buttermilk dressing to taste, scatter with cress and sprouts and season to taste.
WINE SUGGESTION Bright young claret.

SMART-CASUAL LUNCH

SMART-CASUAL LUNCH

ASPARAGUS WITH CAPER AND SHALLOT BUTTER

PREP TIME 5 MINS, COOK 5 MINS
SERVES 6-8

—

24 asparagus spears (about 3 bunches)
100 gm butter, diced
2 golden shallots, finely chopped
1 tbsp salted baby capers, rinsed and drained well
Juice of 1 lemon
Finely grated parmesan, to serve

1 Cook asparagus in a large saucepan of boiling salted water until just tender (2-3 minutes). Drain, then transfer to a plate.
2 Cook butter in a frying pan over high heat until starting to turn nut-brown (1-2 minutes). Remove from heat, add shallot and capers, then lemon juice and spoon sauce onto asparagus. Serve scattered with parmesan.
WINE SUGGESTION Blanc de blancs Champagne.

TOMATO AND BREAD SALAD

Ripe tomatoes with rustic croûtons and creamy Persian feta make for a winning match. Add the croûtons just before serving to preserve their crunch.

PREP TIME 10 MINS, COOK 12 MINS
SERVES 6-8

- 160 gm crustless sourdough bread, torn
- Finely grated rind and juice of 1 lemon, or to taste
- 100 ml extra-virgin olive oil
- 400 gm mixed cherry tomatoes, torn
- 4 large ripe heirloom tomatoes (such as oxheart), cut into thick wedges
- ¼ Spanish onion, thinly sliced
- 1 small garlic clove, finely chopped
- 1 tbsp red wine vinegar
- Large handful each of torn flat-leaf parsley and mint
- 100 gm Persian feta, to serve

1 Preheat oven to 200C. Spread torn bread on an oven tray, scatter with lemon rind, drizzle with 50ml olive oil, season to taste and stir to coat evenly in oil. Bake, stirring occasionally, until golden and toasted (10-12 minutes).

2 Combine tomatoes, onion and garlic in a large bowl, drizzle with vinegar, lemon juice and remaining oil, season to taste and toss to combine, then set aside.

3 Just before serving, add herbs, feta and croûtons to tomatoes, toss to combine and serve.

WINE SUGGESTION Gutsy grenache rosé.

SMART-CASUAL LUNCH

SMART-CASUAL LUNCH

APRICOTS POACHED IN ORANGE MUSCAT WITH MASCARPONE AND ALMONDS

The poaching liquid from the apricots would make a lovely jelly to serve as an accompaniment, but it otherwise keeps for months to reuse for poaching other fruit.

PREP TIME 5 MINS, COOK 10 MINS
SERVES 6-8

—

- 60 gm flaked almonds
- 375 ml (1½ cups) dessert wine (see note)
- 200 gm raw sugar
- 1 vanilla bean, split, seeds scraped
- 12 apricots, halved
- 300 gm each mascarpone, crème fraîche and thickened cream
- 1 tbsp sieved pure icing sugar, or to taste

1 Preheat oven to 170C. Scatter almonds over a tray and roast until light golden (4-6 minutes). Set aside on tray to cool.
2 Meanwhile, bring dessert wine, sugar, vanilla bean and seeds, and 160ml water to the boil over medium-high heat, then reduce heat to medium, add apricots, bring to a simmer (2-3 minutes), then remove from heat and stand apricots in poaching liquid to cool while you serve the meal.
3 To serve, whisk mascarpone, crème fraîche, cream and icing sugar in a bowl to soft peaks. Spoon apricots and a little syrup into bowls and top with the cream and flaked almonds.
NOTE We use Brown Brothers Orange Muscat and Flora; if it's unavailable, substitute another light, sticky white wine.
WINE SUGGESTION The same wine you used for poaching the apricots.

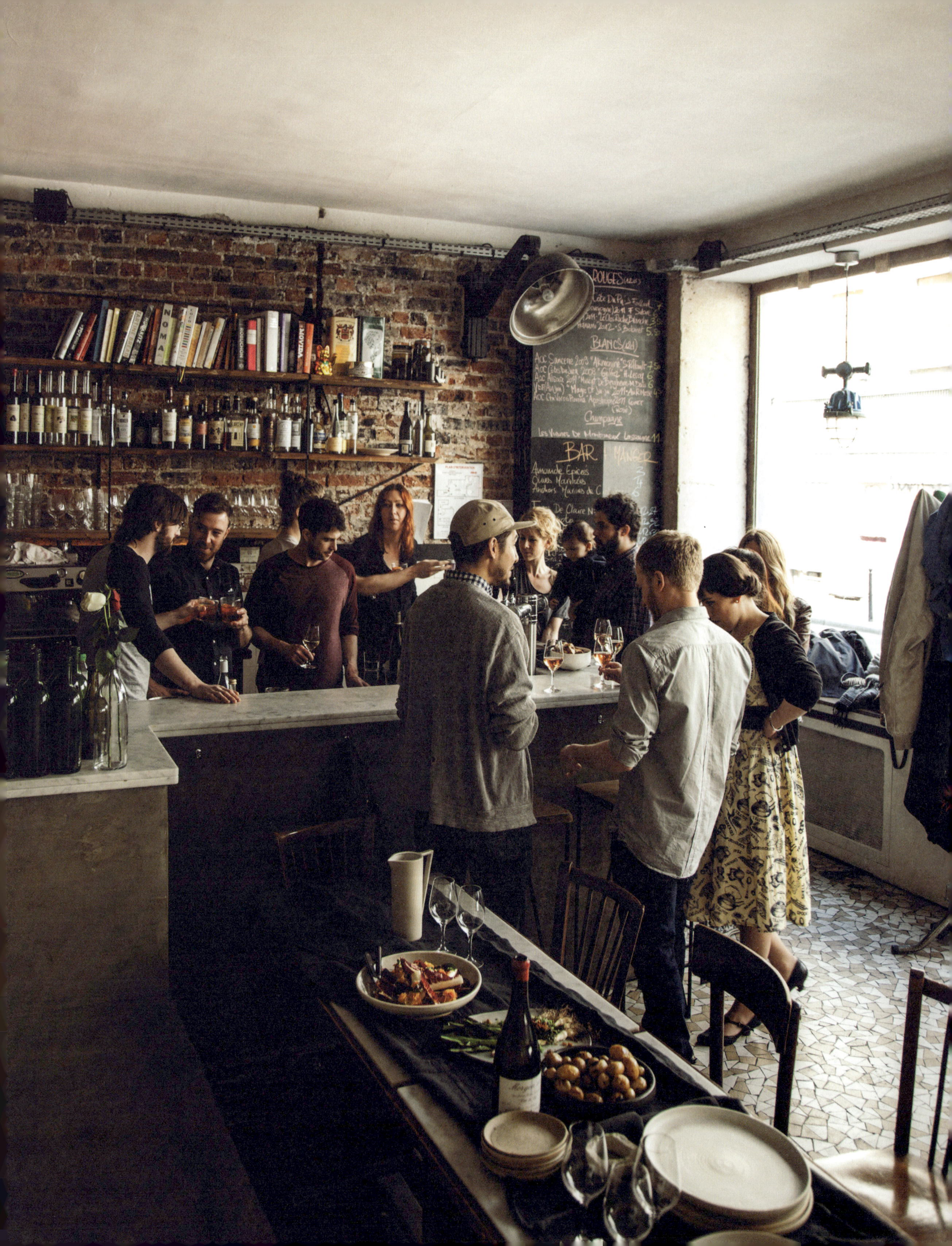
ROUGES
BLANCS
Champagne
BAR
MANGER
NOMA

LUNCH IN PARIS

Lunch in the 11th arrondissement is about as chic as it gets. Chefs James Henry and Shaun Kelly show how it's done with this refined yet relaxed menu that promises next-level results. Crack open the Beaujolais – the party's ready to roll.

—

+ Beetroot soup with burrata

+ Pressed veal head terrine

+ Roast quail with yoghurt and celery

+ Bonito with mojama

+ Slow-roasted lamb with citrus and herbs

+ Roast pumpkin with radicchio, ricotta salata, chilli and lemon

+ Leeks with green sauce

+ Smoked potatoes

+ Goat's yoghurt sorbet with warm burnt honey madeleines

—

BEETROOT SOUP WITH BURRATA

"Beetroot is one of those ingredients that in some form or another ends up on almost every menu I write," says Shaun Kelly. "Its earthiness combines beautifully with creamy burrata."

PREP TIME 25 MINS, COOK 1 HR
SERVES 8

—

- 1 tbsp olive oil
- 1 small Spanish onion, finely chopped
- 2 garlic cloves, finely chopped
- 750 gm (about 4) beetroot, peeled and diced
- 1 medium (200gm) floury potato, such as coliban, peeled and diced
- 1 small fresh bay leaf
- ½ tsp ground cumin
- 1¼ tbsp sherry vinegar
- 500 gm burrata, torn
- Extra-virgin olive oil, to serve

1 Heat oil in a large saucepan over low heat, add onion and garlic and sauté until softened and translucent (5-7 minutes). Add beetroot, potato, bay leaf and cumin, place a round of baking paper directly on surface and cook until beetroot and potato are very tender when pierced with a skewer (35-40 minutes), removing baking paper regularly to stir, especially towards the end of cooking. Add enough water to cover (about 1 litre), season to taste, bring to a simmer and cook until stock is well flavoured (10-12 minutes). Discard bay leaf, process soup in a blender until smooth, add sherry vinegar and season to taste. Divide among serving bowls, top with torn burrata, drizzle with extra-virgin olive oil, scatter with pepper and serve hot.
WINE SUGGESTION Young juicy red Beaujolais.

LUNCH IN PARIS

LUNCH IN PARIS

PRESSED VEAL HEAD TERRINE

"The garnish here is my loose version of a classic gribiche," says James Henry. Veal head isn't readily available in Australia, but it can be ordered from specialist butchers. Ask them to clean and quarter the head for you; otherwise substitute veal cheeks and tongue. The terrine is large enough to serve a crowd, or it will keep for up to a week in the refrigerator. Begin this recipe three days ahead to brine the veal head and set the terrine.

PREP TIME 1 HR, COOK 3¼ HRS (PLUS COOLING, PRESSING)
SERVES 16

—

- 1 kg sea salt
- 1 veal head (about 6kg), cleaned and quartered
- 2 onions, coarsely chopped
- 2 carrots, coarsely chopped
- 2 celery stalks, coarsely chopped
- 2 fresh bay leaves
- 2 tsp Dijon mustard
- 4 eggs, at room temperature
- Extra-virgin olive oil, chervil sprigs, fennel tops and mayonnaise, to serve
- 40 gm (⅓ cup) cornichons, finely chopped
- 50 gm (⅓ cup) salted capers, rinsed and finely chopped

1 Stir salt and 2 litres water in a stockpot over low heat until salt dissolves, then remove from heat and add 8 litres cold water. Cool completely.

2 Rinse the quarters of veal head under cold running water and divide between two 10-litre non-reactive containers (see cook's notes p279). Add enough brine to cover completely, weight with a plate to keep submerged, cover and refrigerate for 2 days.

3 Drain the veal head (discard brine), rinse thoroughly and place in a stockpot. Add onion, carrot, celery and bay leaves, and cover completely with cold water. Bring to the boil, skim impurities from the surface, reduce heat to low-medium and simmer, skimming occasionally, until meat is falling from the bone (2½-3 hours). Cool head in stock; to speed up this process, place stockpot in a sink of cold water, replacing the water after 30 minutes. When the head is cool enough to handle, remove from stock (reserve), shred the meat and set aside (discard skin and bones).

4 Strain cooking liquid, then simmer 500ml cooking liquid in a large frying pan over high heat until reduced by half (5-6 minutes; discard remaining liquid and vegetables). Be careful not to over-reduce or it will become too salty. Strain through a fine sieve, whisk in Dijon mustard and set aside to cool.

5 Spoon the meat into an oiled 7.5cm-deep, 23cm x 10cm terrine mould. Place on a tray to catch any drips, pour in enough reduced cooking liquid to cover meat, cover with plastic wrap, then weight with food cans and refrigerate overnight to set.

6 On the day of serving, cook eggs in boiling water until hard-boiled (10 minutes), drain, cool under cold running water and peel. Separate yolks from whites, push yolks through a fine sieve, finely chop whites, and set yolks and whites aside separately.

7 Turn terrine out onto a platter or board and thickly slice. Place slices on serving plates, drizzle with extra-virgin olive oil, scatter with herbs and serve with eggwhite, egg yolk, mayonnaise, cornichons and capers.

DRINK SUGGESTION Rustic cider from Brittany.

ROAST QUAIL WITH YOGHURT AND CELERY

"The whey that drains from yoghurt when you hang it makes a great brine," says Kelly. "It doesn't need to be very salty – the brine's main purpose is to keep the quail juicy. And the birds are great either roasted or barbecued." Begin this recipe two days ahead to drain the yoghurt and marinate the quail.

PREP TIME 30 MINS, COOK 20 MINS (PLUS DRAINING, BRINING, DRYING)
SERVES 8

—

- 1 kg Greek-style yoghurt
- 2 tbsp olive oil
- 4½ tsp sea salt flakes
- 8 fresh bay leaves
- 8 garlic cloves, bruised
- 2 tsp coarsely ground white pepper
- 8 quail (about 200gm each)
- 2 celery stalks, leaves picked
- 4 lemons, halved

1 Place yoghurt in a muslin-lined colander over a bowl, cover and refrigerate until whey has drained and yoghurt is thick (24 hours). Reserve whey and yoghurt separately in refrigerator until required.

2 Combine whey, 1 tbsp olive oil, 3 tsp sea salt flakes, bay leaves, garlic and white pepper in a non-reactive container (see cook's notes p279) to make a light brine. Add quail, cover and refrigerate overnight to marinate.

3 Meanwhile, spread celery leaves on an oven tray and dry out in the oven at lowest setting (3 hours to overnight). Process with remaining sea salt flakes in a small food processor or pound using a mortar and pestle until finely ground. Store in an airtight container until required.

4 Preheat oven to 220C. Remove quail from brine, pat dry with paper towels and place a bay leaf and a garlic clove from the brine into the cavity of each quail (discard brine). Place in a lightly oiled roasting pan, drizzle with remaining oil and roast until golden and just cooked through (15-20 minutes).

5 Meanwhile, cook lemon halves, cut-side down, in a large frying pan (with no oil) over medium-high heat until just starting to char (2 minutes), then transfer to pan with quail halfway through cooking.

6 Juice celery, strain the juice and stir into the drained yoghurt to thin it slightly.

7 Serve roast quail with burnt lemon, a dollop of yoghurt, and celery salt.

WINE SUGGESTION Mineral-rich chenin blanc.

LUNCH IN PARIS

JAMES HENRY
(LEFT) &
SHAUN KELLY

106 GOURMET TRAVELLER | MENUS

LUNCH IN PARIS

LUNCH IN PARIS

BONITO WITH MOJAMA

"I love bonito for this recipe, but you could substitute mackerel or another semi-oily fish, as long as it's super-fresh," says Henry. You'll need a blowtorch to achieve the combination of caramelised exterior and rare flesh; it's difficult to replicate this effect with a griller.

PREP TIME 20 MINS, COOK 5 MINS (PLUS CURING, MARINATING)
SERVES 8

—

- 1.6 kg bonito, filleted, skinned, pin bones and blood line removed, cut into 10cm lengths
- 75 gm (⅓ cup) caster sugar
- 75 gm (⅓ cup) sea salt
- 1 Spanish onion, quartered, petals separated
- 400 ml buttermilk
- 80 ml (⅓ cup) ponzu
- Mojama (see note), toasted sesame oil and baby wood sorrel leaves, to serve

1 Place fish in a non-reactive container (see cook's notes p279). Combine sugar and salt in a bowl, then scatter mixture over both sides of fish, cover and refrigerate for 3 hours to cure.
2 Blanch onion until just tender (30 seconds; see cook's notes p279), refresh and drain well. Place in a non-reactive container with buttermilk and ponzu and marinate for 1 hour.
3 Brush cure mixture from fish and transfer fish to a foil-lined oven tray. Lightly caramelise with a blowtorch and divide among serving plates.
4 Drain onion (reserve marinade), scatter onto bonito, then finely grate mojama over the top. Drizzle with a little buttermilk marinade and sesame oil, scatter with sorrel leaves and serve.
NOTE Mojama, dried cured tuna, is available from Spanish delicatessens.
WINE SUGGESTION Skin-contact sauvignon blanc.

SLOW-ROASTED LAMB WITH CITRUS AND HERBS

This simplest of dishes relies on quality lamb. James Henry uses a whole milk-fed lamb from the Pyrénées, but the method is equally good applied to a shoulder. It's important to bring the meat to room temperature before cooking it.

PREP TIME 15 MINS, COOK 1¾ HRS
SERVES 8

—

2.3	kg piece lamb shoulder, bone in
	Olive oil, for rubbing
150	gm butter, coarsely chopped
2	garlic cloves, bruised
2	fresh bay leaves
3	thyme sprigs
	Thinly peeled rind of 1 orange and 1 lemon

1 Preheat oven to 140C. Place lamb on an oven tray, rub with a little oil and season to taste.
2 Melt butter in a small saucepan over medium heat, add garlic, bay leaves, thyme and orange rind, then remove from heat and season to taste. Brush lamb with a little butter mixture, then roast, basting frequently with remaining butter mixture, until tender (1¼-1½ hours). Increase oven to 200C and roast lamb until well browned (12-15 minutes). Serve hot drizzled with buttery juices.
WINE SUGGESTION Spicy red Côtes du Rhône.

LUNCH IN PARIS

LUNCH IN PARIS

ROAST PUMPKIN WITH RADICCHIO, RICOTTA SALATA, CHILLI AND LEMON

"We use potimarron, a small pear-shaped pumpkin with subtle chestnut flavours," says Henry, *"but you can use butternut pumpkin instead."*

PREP TIME 15 MINS, COOK 1¼ HRS
SERVES 8

—

- 1 butternut pumpkin (1.5kg), quartered, seeds removed
- 1½ tbsp olive oil
- 1 radicchio di Treviso, leaves separated
- ⅔ cup (loosely packed) mint
- Finely grated ricotta salata, chilli flakes and lemon wedges, to serve

1 Preheat oven to 200C. Place pumpkin in a roasting pan, drizzle with oil and season to taste with salt. Roast until tender and dark golden (1-1¼ hours), then coarsely tear and place in a bowl. Add radicchio and mint, scatter with ricotta and chilli flakes, squeeze lemon over to taste, toss to combine and serve warm.

114 GOURMET TRAVELLER | MENUS

LUNCH IN PARIS

LEEKS WITH GREEN SAUCE

"If you can't find baby leeks, you're probably better off using spring onions," says Kelly. "You can serve the green sauce the same day you make it, but it's even better made a couple of days ahead to round out the flavours. I like to cook the leeks on the barbecue, although you could blanch them quickly and cook them in a char-grill pan instead."

PREP TIME 25 MINS, COOK 15 MINS
SERVES 8

—

- 90 gm coarse fresh white breadcrumbs
- 5 tsp olive oil
- 2 large bunches baby (pencil) leeks
- Lemon wedges, to serve

GREEN SAUCE

- 125 ml (½ cup) olive oil
- ½ cup (loosely packed) flat-leaf parsley, plus extra to serve
- ½ cup (loosely packed) mint, plus extra to serve
- ½ cup (loosely packed) chervil, plus extra to serve
- ¼ cup (loosely packed) dill, plus extra to serve
- 1 tbsp (loosely packed) tarragon, plus extra to serve
- 15 (45gm) anchovy fillets, finely chopped
- 2 tsp salted capers, rinsed
- 1 small garlic clove, finely chopped

1 For the green sauce, pour a good glug of the oil into a bowl and place next to your chopping board. Finely chop the herbs, leaving a little texture, and place them straight into the oil so they don't lose their goodness. Add anchovies, capers and garlic, mix well and season to taste – the anchovies should take care of the salt, but add a healthy grind of pepper. Add remaining oil, or enough to form a drizzling consistency (you may not need it all), cover and refrigerate until required.
2 Preheat oven to 180C. Mix breadcrumbs and 3 tsp oil in a bowl, season to taste, spread on an oven tray and bake, stirring occasionally, until toasted and golden (10-12 minutes). Stand to cool.
3 Heat a barbecue to high. Wash and trim the leeks, leaving a good amount of green on, and the roots, too, if they're not too dirty. Drizzle with remaining oil and barbecue in batches, turning once, until charred and wilted (1-2 minutes each side). Serve hot with a good helping of green sauce, a sprinkle of toasted breadcrumbs, extra herbs and a squeeze of lemon.

SMOKED POTATOES

PREP TIME 10 MINS, COOK 1 HR
SERVES 8

—

- 1.2 kg baby Nicola or cream delight potatoes, scrubbed
- 3 thyme sprigs
- 1 garlic clove, bruised
- 1 fresh bay leaf
- 100 gm hay (see note)
- Melted butter, to serve

1 Place potatoes, thyme, garlic and bay leaf in a saucepan, cover with plenty of salted cold water, bring to the boil, then reduce heat to low-medium and simmer until just tender when pierced with a skewer (25-30 minutes). Drain and set aside.
2 Spread hay in the base of a flameproof casserole lined with foil (smoking may stain the pan) and place a round wire rack on top of the hay. Spread potatoes on rack, cover with a lid and place casserole over high heat until hay starts to smoke (3-4 minutes). Reduce heat to low and smoke until potatoes are tender and well flavoured (30 minutes). Drizzle with melted butter, season to taste and serve hot.
NOTE Hay is available from large pet stores.

LUNCH IN PARIS

LUNCH IN PARIS

GOAT'S YOGHURT SORBET WITH WARM BURNT HONEY MADELEINES

"Goat's yoghurt sorbet is one of my favourites because it's so versatile," says Henry. "I sometimes serve it with my version of a carrot cake, or with something as simple as strawberries and crisp clove meringue. We make our own goat's milk yoghurt, but a good shop-bought one works well, too. When you're making the madeleines, make sure you caramelise the honey well; otherwise the madeleines will be too sweet." Begin this recipe two days ahead to drain the yoghurt.

PREP TIME 1 HR, COOK 25 MINS (PLUS DRAINING, FREEZING)
MAKES 24

—

- 90 gm honey
- 100 gm butter, coarsely chopped, plus extra, melted, for brushing
- 70 gm blanched almonds
- 2 eggs
- 25 gm caster sugar
- Finely grated rind of ½ lemon
- 50 gm (⅓ cup) plain flour
- ¼ tsp baking powder
- Extra-virgin olive oil and thyme leaves, to serve

GOAT'S YOGHURT SORBET
- 1 kg goat's milk yoghurt
- 250 ml (1 cup) goat's milk
- 250 ml (1 cup) pouring cream
- 175 gm caster sugar
- 1 tbsp liquid glucose
- Zested rind of 1 lemon
- ½ tsp dried lavender (see note)

1 For goat's yoghurt sorbet, place yoghurt in a muslin-lined colander over a bowl, cover and refrigerate until whey has drained and yoghurt is very thick (36 hours; discard whey). Combine remaining ingredients in a saucepan and heat to just below simmering, stirring to dissolve sugar. Set aside to cool and infuse (about 1 hour), then strain into a bowl and whisk in drained yoghurt. Churn in an ice-cream machine and freeze until required. This sorbet is best eaten on the day it's churned. Makes about 1.5 litres.

2 Simmer honey in a small saucepan over medium-high heat until caramelised (2-3 minutes; be careful, honey will froth up). Dip the base of the saucepan quickly in cold water to stop cooking, then keep the honey warm.

3 Heat butter in a saucepan over medium-high heat, swirling pan occasionally, until nut brown (3-4 minutes). Dip the base of the saucepan quickly in cold water to stop cooking, then keep the butter warm.

4 Process almonds in a food processor until finely ground, then set aside.

5 Whisk eggs, sugar, lemon rind and a pinch of salt in an electric mixer until pale and fluffy (3-4 minutes), then gradually pour in warm honey, whisking to combine. Sieve in flour and baking powder, add ground almonds and fold to combine, then fold in warm butter. The madeleine batter can be made 2 days ahead and refrigerated until required.

6 Preheat oven to 180C. Brush large madeleine moulds with melted butter, spoon 1 tbsp batter into each (don't overfill) and bake until golden and puffed (5-7 minutes). Remove madeleines from moulds, wipe out moulds and repeat with remaining batter. Serve madeleines warm with goat's yoghurt sorbet drizzled with extra-virgin olive oil and scattered with thyme leaves.

NOTE Dried lavender is available from Herbie's Spices (herbies.com.au). Madeleine moulds are available from select cookware shops.

WINE SUGGESTION Rich late-harvest pinot gris.

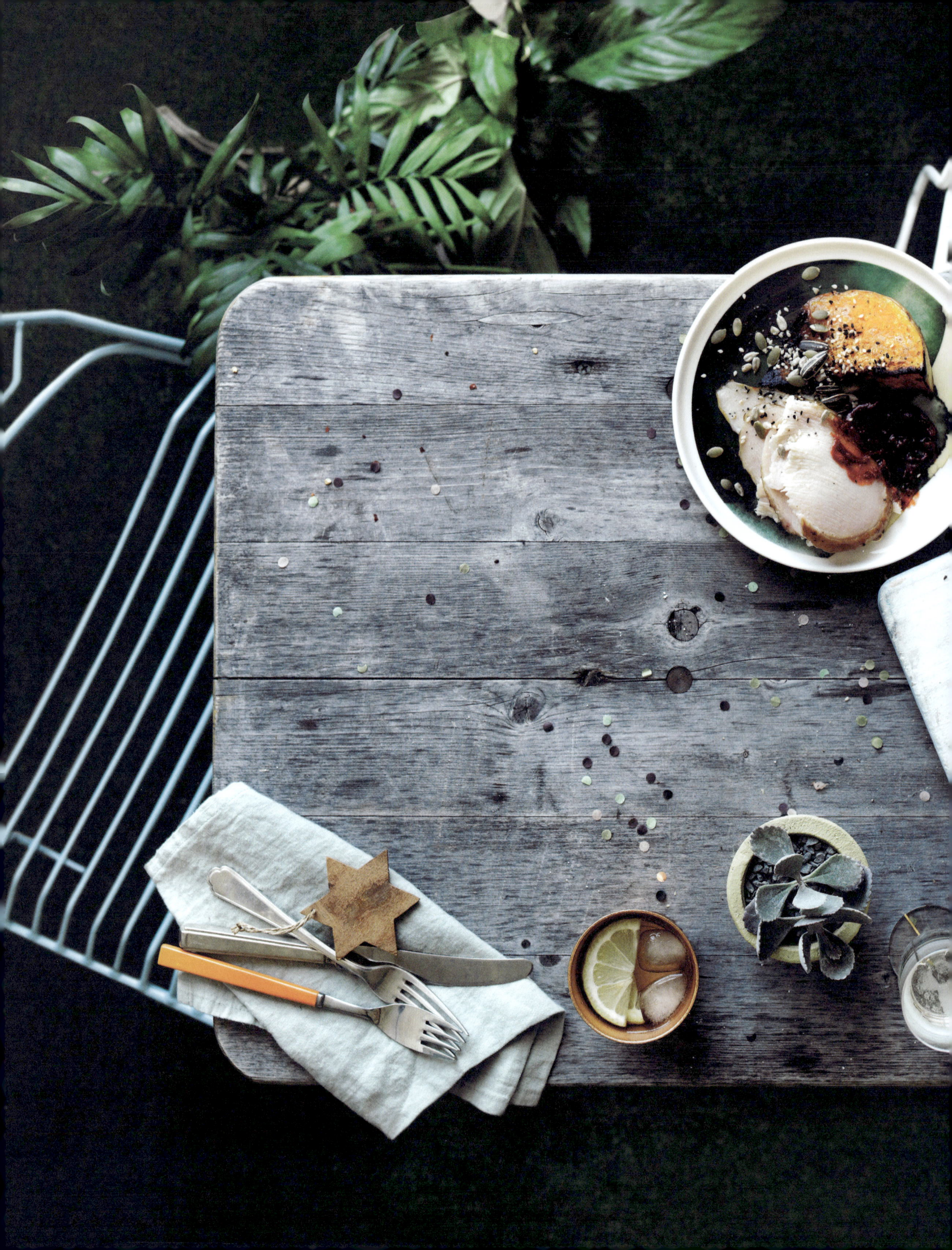

CHRISTMAS ALFRESCO

Take your Christmas outside with a lunch menu full of festive hits. Most of the work is done ahead so by the time you're at the table the only thing you'll need to worry about is keeping the glasses full. It's Christmas Down Under, and we love it.

—

+ Chilled corn soup with yabbies

+ Pea and ham salad

+ Cider-brined smoked turkey with cranberry barbecue sauce

+ Roast pumpkin with thyme and lemon butter, and spiced seeds

+ Green peppercorn beef with caraway cream

+ Cauliflower salad with orange and cumin dressing, and buffalo yoghurt

+ Cherry lattice pie with almond-milk ice

—

CHILLED CORN SOUP WITH YABBIES

The yabbies can be prepared ahead and the soup assembled just before serving. Take the soup out of the fridge about half an hour beforehand to take the edge off the chill.

PREP 30 MINS, COOK 1 HR 50 MINS (PLUS CHILLING)
SERVES 6-8

—

- 6 corn cobs, kernels removed, cobs and kernels reserved separately
- 500 ml (2 cups) pouring cream
- 2 thyme sprigs
- 1 garlic clove, crushed
- 50 gm butter, coarsely chopped
- 1 onion, finely chopped
- 12 live yabbies
- 3 tbsp small basil leaves, plus extra to serve
- Juice and finely grated rind of 1 lemon
- Extra-virgin olive oil, to serve

1 To make a corn stock, place corn cobs in a saucepan with 2 litres of water, bring to the boil, then reduce heat to low and simmer for 1 hour. Strain and discard cobs. Makes about 1.5 litres.
2 Combine cream, thyme and garlic in a small saucepan over medium heat and simmer to reduce by half (20-30 minutes). Season to taste, remove thyme and set aside.
3 Melt butter in a saucepan over medium heat. Add onion, sauté until softened and translucent (6-7 minutes), then add corn and cook, stirring occasionally, until starting to soften (3-4 minutes). Add 750ml of corn stock (freeze remaining stock for another use), simmer until kernels are tender (10-12 minutes), then add reserved cream and purée in a blender until smooth. Season to taste, strain into a bowl, cool to room temperature, then refrigerate to chill (1 hour).
4 Kill yabbies humanely (see cook's notes p279). Bring a saucepan of salted water to the boil, add yabbies and cook until just orange (1-2 minutes). Drain, then refresh in iced water and drain again. Working with a yabby at a time, hold and lift the middle flap on the tail and lightly twist from side to side to loosen. Carefully remove tail flap, pulling out the intestinal tract with it. Twist the tail and head in opposite directions to separate, then remove tail meat from shell and place on a tray lined with paper towels. Refrigerate until required.
5 To serve, coarsely chop yabby meat and combine in a bowl with basil and lemon juice and rind, season to taste, divide among bowls of corn soup, scatter with extra basil leaves and cracked black pepper, and drizzle with olive oil.
DRINK SUGGESTION An aromatic hoppy IPA.

CHRISTMAS ALFRESCO

CHRISTMAS ALFRESCO

PEA AND HAM SALAD

This is a twist on the traditional pairing of pea and ham – a more festive, summer version. It's also a great way to use leftover ham.

PREP TIME 25 MINS, COOK 1 HR 10 MINS
SERVES 6

—

- 1 picnic ham (about 4.5kg; see note)
- 300 gm each sugar snap peas and snow peas, trimmed, reserving tendrils to serve
- 200 gm frozen peas
- 2 tbsp tarragon, torn
- 1 cup (loosely packed) mint, torn
- 60 ml (¼ cup) extra-virgin olive oil
- 40 ml (2 tbsp) sherry vinegar

SHERRY VINEGAR, QUINCE AND MUSTARD GLAZE
- 100 ml sherry vinegar
- 100 gm quince paste, coarsely chopped
- 80 gm brown sugar
- 1 tbsp Dijon mustard

1 Preheat oven to 180C. For sherry vinegar, quince and mustard glaze, simmer ingredients and 100ml water in a small saucepan over low heat, stirring frequently, until a thick glaze forms (6-8 minutes). Remove from heat and set aside.

2 Gently peel back the skin of the ham from the leg to the shank, being careful not to tear the fat, then use a sharp knife to score the skin around the shank and remove it in a single piece. Reserve. Score the fat diagonally across the leg at 2cm intervals and repeat scoring in the opposite direction to create a diamond pattern. Place ham in a roasting pan, brush with glaze, pour water into pan to a depth of 1cm and roast, basting occasionally, until deep golden and warmed through (50 minutes to 1 hour). Cool briefly, then cut 12 thick slices and coarsely chop. Leftover ham will keep for a week covered in the fridge.

3 Blanch sugar snaps and snow peas until bright green (30 seconds to 1 minute; see cook's notes p279), drain and refresh, and drain again. Blanch peas until bright green (1-1½ minutes), drain and refresh, and drain again. Combine in a large bowl with herbs, ham, olive oil and sherry vinegar, season to taste and serve topped with snow pea tendrils.

NOTE A picnic ham is smaller than a regular ham. Order it ahead from your butcher.
WINE SUGGESTION A fruity rosé.

CIDER-BRINED SMOKED TURKEY
WITH CRANBERRY BARBECUE SAUCE

ROAST PUMPKIN WITH THYME AND
LEMON BUTTER, AND SPICED SEEDS

CHRISTMAS ALFRESCO

CIDER-BRINED SMOKED TURKEY WITH CRANBERRY BARBECUE SAUCE

You'll need a kettle-style barbecue for this outdoors take on the classic turkey-and-cranberry combo. Begin this recipe two days ahead to brine the turkey.

PREP TIME 45 MINS, COOK 4 HRS (PLUS RESTING)
SERVES 6-8

—

- 300 gm sea salt
- 300 gm brown sugar
- 4 garlic cloves, crushed
- 2 rosemary sprigs
- 2 tsp black peppercorns, crushed
- 2 dried bay leaves
- 750 ml apple cider
- 60 ml (¼ cup) apple cider vinegar
- 1 turkey (about 4kg)
- 40 gm butter, softened
- 200 gm wood chunks such as cherry or apple (see note)

CRANBERRY BARBECUE SAUCE

- 2 tbsp olive oil
- 1 Spanish onion, finely chopped
- 3 garlic cloves, finely chopped
- 2 tbsp tomato paste
- 200 gm frozen cranberries
- 130 gm brown sugar
- 125 ml (½ cup) apple cider vinegar
- 70 ml Worcestershire sauce
- 2 tbsp Dijon mustard
- Pinch each of ground chilli and allspice
- 20 gm butter, coarsely chopped

1 Stir salt, sugar, garlic, rosemary, peppercorns, bay leaves and 4 litres of water in a large saucepan over medium heat to dissolve sugar and salt (2-3 minutes). Cool to room temperature, then add cider and cider vinegar and stir to combine. Rinse turkey under cold running water, pat dry with paper towels and place in a non-reactive container (see cook's notes p279) large enough to submerge turkey in brine. Pour in brine, weigh down turkey with a plate to keep it submerged and refrigerate for 2 days. Rinse off brine under cold running water and pat dry with paper towels. Starting at the neck end of the bird, gently work your fingers under the skin to separate it from the flesh, being careful not to tear it, then carefully push butter under skin and evenly over breasts. Smooth over the top to spread butter evenly. Season to taste with salt and cracked black pepper.

2 For cranberry barbecue sauce, heat oil in a saucepan over medium heat, add onion and garlic and sauté until tender and onion is translucent (6-8 minutes). Add tomato paste and stir until it darkens slightly (1-2 minutes). Add remaining ingredients except butter and simmer until thick and dark in colour (20-25 minutes). Remove from heat, cool briefly, then add butter and process using a hand-held blender or food processor until smooth. Season to taste.

3 Prepare a large kettle barbecue for indirect grilling. Push coals to one side and place a drip tray under the grill to catch the juices. Place turkey on the grill over the tray and scatter a few soaked medium-sized wood chunks (see note) over coals, cover with barbecue lid and cook, basting occasionally, until cooked through (3½-4 hours). You may need to add more coals and wood during cooking. Aim to keep the grill at around 120C. Cover turkey loosely with foil and rest in a warm place for around 30 minutes, then carve and serve with cranberry barbecue sauce.

NOTE Chunks of wood for smoking are available from barbecue shops. Pick out the medium-sized pieces and soak them in cold water for at least an hour before use.

DRINK SUGGESTION Bottle-fermented Australian cider.

ROAST PUMPKIN WITH THYME AND LEMON BUTTER, AND SPICED SEEDS

Roast pumpkin has a wonderful flavour at room temperature and the spiced seeds add a lovely crunch.

PREP TIME 20 MINS, COOK 1 HR
SERVES 6-8

—

- 1 butternut pumpkin (about 2kg), cut into wedges
- 2 tbsp extra-virgin olive oil
- 2 tbsp thyme leaves
- 80 gm butter, coarsely chopped
- Finely grated rind of 1 lemon and juice of 2

SPICED SEED MIX
- 50 gm (¼ cup) pumpkin seed kernels
- 35 gm (¼ cup) sunflower seed kernels
- 2 tbsp each black and white sesame seeds
- 1 tbsp caraway seeds
- 1 tsp smoked paprika

1 Preheat oven to 190C. Combine pumpkin, oil and half the thyme in a roasting pan. Season to taste and roast, turning occasionally, until golden and caramelised (50 minutes to 1 hour). Cool to room temperature.

2 For spiced seed mix, dry-roast pumpkin seeds and sunflower seeds in a frying pan until golden (1 minute; see cook's notes p279), then set aside. Dry-roast remaining seeds until golden (30 seconds to 1 minute), then toss all the seeds together along with paprika.

3 Heat butter in a small saucepan over low heat until light golden (2-3 minutes), remove from heat, add lemon rind and juice, then transfer to a small bowl and add remaining thyme.

4 Serve pumpkin at room temperature drizzled with warm thyme and lemon butter and scattered with spiced seed mix.

WINE SUGGESTION A perfumed, rich white viognier.

CHRISTMAS ALFRESCO

GREEN PEPPERCORN BEEF WITH CARAWAY CREAM

Here's a simple and delicious way to serve beef. Cook it on the barbecue if you're having a full outdoor Christmas – just be sure to leave enough time for it to cool to room temperature, which is when it's at its best.

PREP TIME 20 MINS, COOK 45 MINS (PLUS RESTING)
SERVES 6-8

—

- 1 beef fillet (about 1.6kg), trimmed of sinew
- 70 ml olive oil
- 35 gm (¼ cup) dried green peppercorns, coarsely ground

CARAWAY CREAM

- 2 tbsp caraway seeds
- 200 gm crème fraîche
- 2 tbsp rosemary, coarsely chopped, plus extra to serve
- 1 tbsp finely grated horseradish, or horseradish purée
- Finely grated rind and juice of ½ lemon

1 Preheat oven to 160C. Truss beef at 3cm intervals with kitchen string. Brush with 2 tbsp oil and roll in ground peppercorns, pressing so they stick. Heat remaining oil in a large frying pan over high heat, add beef and sear it, turning occasionally, until brown (1-2 minutes each side). Place on a wire rack over a roasting tray and roast in oven until cooked to your liking (35-40 minutes for rare). Cover loosely with foil then set aside to rest and cool to room temperature.

2 For caraway cream, dry-roast caraway seeds in a frying pan over medium heat until fragrant (30 seconds; see cook's notes p279). Pound using a mortar and pestle until coarsely crushed. Cool, then combine in a bowl with remaining ingredients, season to taste, top with extra rosemary and serve with thickly sliced beef.

WINE SUGGESTION A young Coonawarra cabernet.

CAULIFLOWER SALAD WITH ORANGE AND CUMIN DRESSING, AND BUFFALO YOGHURT

Raw cauliflower is fantastic in a salad, making for extreme crunch. Make sure you give it enough time in the dressing to soak up the flavours. Begin this recipe a day ahead to drain the yoghurt.

PREP TIME 25 MINS, COOK 5 MINS (PLUS DRAINING)
SERVES 6-8

—

- 500 gm buffalo yoghurt (see note)
- ½ cauliflower (about 400gm), broken into florets
- 2 each purple and orange carrots, thinly sliced into ribbons on a mandolin
- 1 cup (loosely packed) flat-leaf parsley
- ½ cup (loosely packed) dill
- 50 gm pistachio kernels, coarsely chopped
- Extra-virgin olive oil and chilli flakes, to serve

ORANGE AND CUMIN DRESSING
- 1 tsp cumin seeds
- 100 ml extra-virgin olive oil
- 80 ml (⅓ cup) orange juice
- 60 ml (¼ cup) lemon juice
- 1 tbsp red wine vinegar
- ½ tsp honey

1 Place buffalo yoghurt in a colander or sieve lined with muslin, then place over a bowl to drain, cover and refrigerate overnight until thick (discard liquid).
2 For orange and cumin dressing, dry-roast cumin seeds (30 seconds; see cook's notes p279), then crush using a mortar and pestle. Transfer to a bowl, add remaining ingredients, whisk to combine and season to taste.
3 Combine cauliflower and carrot in a large bowl, add dressing, toss to combine, season to taste and set aside until carrot starts to soften (3-5 minutes). Add herbs, reserving some for garnish, toss to combine, then scatter with pistachios and reserved herbs. Drizzle buffalo yoghurt with extra-virgin olive oil, scatter with chilli flakes, and serve with salad.
NOTE Buffalo yoghurt is available from select delicatessens and grocers. Sheep's milk or Greek-style yoghurt make great substitutes.
WINE SUGGESTION Spanish verdejo.

CHRISTMAS ALFRESCO

CHRISTMAS ALFRESCO

CHERRY LATTICE PIE WITH ALMOND-MILK ICE

This pie is best served at room temperature, ensuring the cherry filling has a lovely jammy texture. Use good unsweetened almond milk for the ice.

PREP TIME 1 HR, COOK 1 HR 10 MINS (PLUS FREEZING, RESTING)
SERVES 6-8

—

- 1.2 kg cherries, pitted
- 600 gm frozen sour cherries, defrosted (see note)
- 200 gm caster sugar
- 60 gm almond meal
- 35 gm cornflour
- 1 vanilla bean, split, seeds scraped
- Finely grated rind of ½ lemon
- 10 gm butter, coarsely chopped
- 1 egg lightly beaten with 1 tbsp milk, for eggwash
- Demerara sugar, for scattering

ALMOND-MILK ICE
- 750 ml (3 cups) almond milk (see note)
- 55 gm (¼ cup) raw caster sugar
- 1 tbsp honey
- 1 cinnamon quill
- 1 vanilla bean, split, seeds scraped
- Finely grated rind of 1 orange
- Splash of brandy (optional)

CINNAMON PASTRY
- 350 gm (2⅓ cups) plain flour
- 225 gm chilled butter, coarsely chopped
- 1 tbsp caster sugar, plus extra to garnish
- ½ tsp ground cinnamon

1 For almond-milk ice, stir ingredients in a saucepan over medium heat to dissolve sugar and honey, then set aside to cool. Pour into a tray and freeze, scraping with a fork every 30 minutes to form ice crystals, until mixture is completely frozen. Just before serving, scrape with a fork again to loosen the ice crystals.

2 For cinnamon pastry, pulse flour, butter, sugar, cinnamon and a large pinch of salt in a food processor until half combined. Add 80ml iced water and process until pastry just comes together. Turn out onto a lightly floured surface and bring together. Divide in half, form into discs, wrap each half in plastic wrap and refrigerate for 2 hours to rest.

3 Meanwhile, place fresh and frozen cherries, sugar, almond meal, cornflour, vanilla bean and seeds, and lemon rind in a bowl, and toss to combine.

4 Preheat oven to 180C. Roll out a disc of pastry on a lightly floured surface to 5mm thick, place it in a 24cm-diameter pie dish and trim the edges. Roll out remaining pastry to 5mm thick and cut into 2cm-wide strips. Transfer cherry mixture to pastry case, dot with butter and weave pastry strips on top to create a lattice pattern. Brush with eggwash, scatter with sugar, and bake until golden and cooked through (1-1¼ hours). Cool to room temperature and serve with almond-milk ice.

NOTE Frozen sour cherries are available from supermarkets and select delicatessens. If they're unavailable, substitute fresh pitted cherries and add 1 tbsp lemon juice to the filling. Almond milk is available from supermarkets and health-food shops.

WINE SUGGESTION A sparkling Italian brachetto.

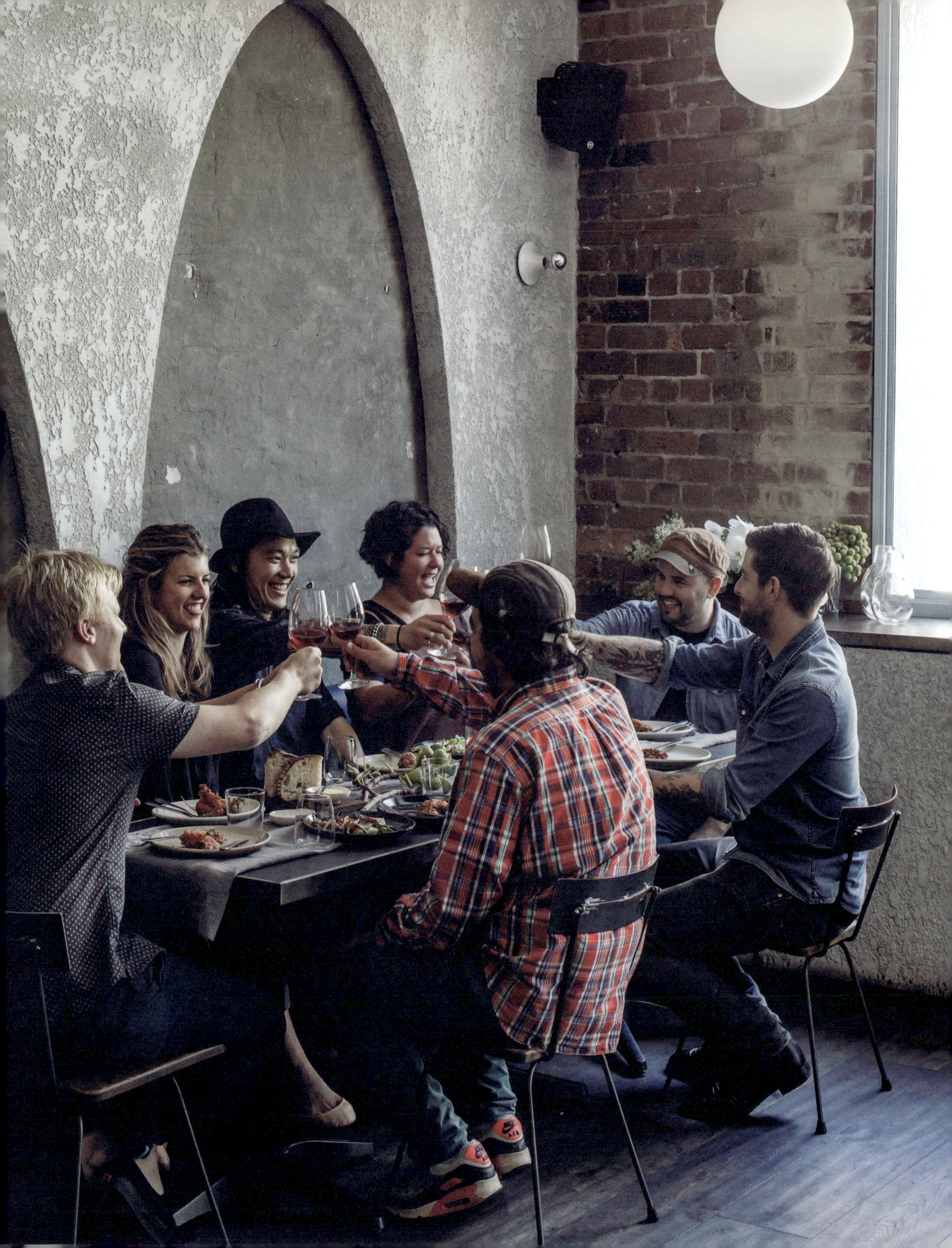

EASTER AT ESTER

Easter is a fine time to get friends around the table and this menu from Mat Lindsay of Sydney's Ester shows there's no need to be a slave to tradition. Gather your nearest and dearest for this selection of dishes that hit the sweet-spot between hip and hearty. Fried rabbit anyone?

—

+ Roast oysters with horseradish

+ Fried rabbit

+ Roast carrots with honey, sesame and parmesan

+ Roast spatchcock with garlic-bread sauce

+ Broccolini with chilli and burnt-garlic vinaigrette

+ Baked apples with burnt cream

+ Salted-caramel semifreddo

—

ROAST OYSTERS WITH HORSERADISH

"I think of these oysters as a good entry level for people who think they don't like oysters," says Mat Lindsay. *"As they're gently warmed through, the oysters poach in their own briny juices and the texture becomes less slippery. You can use whatever oyster is the best when you're buying, of course, but I have a soft spot for a good Sydney rock."*

PREP TIME 10 MINS, COOK 15 MINS
SERVES 6-8

—

Rock salt, for roasting
1½ dozen unshucked oysters, scrubbed

HORSERADISH DRESSING
80 ml (⅓ cup) brown rice vinegar
1 tbsp finely grated horseradish
1 golden shallot, finely chopped

1 Preheat oven on its highest setting. Cover the base of a roasting pan large enough to fit oysters in a single layer with a 1cm layer of rock salt and place in the oven to warm the salt (5-10 minutes). Arrange unopened oysters on the salt and roast until lids pop open slightly (2-3 minutes).
2 For horseradish dressing, combine ingredients and season to taste with freshly ground black pepper.
3 To serve, remove top shells from oysters (the oysters should be just warm and plumped up a little). Spoon a little horseradish dressing over each oyster and serve straightaway.
WINE SUGGESTION A full-bodied dry sake.

EASTER AT ESTER

140 GOURMET TRAVELLER | MENUS

MAT LINDSAY

EASTER AT ESTER

FRIED RABBIT

"When I was coming up with this menu I had to ask myself if it's really okay to eat the Easter bunny," says Lindsay. "I say yes – especially when it tastes this good." Start this recipe a day ahead to marinate the rabbit.

PREP TIME 20 MINS, COOK 10 MINS (PLUS MARINATING)
SERVES 6-8

—

- 1 rabbit, jointed into 8 pieces
- 500 ml (2 cups) buttermilk (see note)
- 150 gm gochujang (see note)
- Vegetable oil, for deep-frying
- Lemon cheeks, to serve

CRUMB COATING
- 300 gm (2 cups) plain flour
- 60 gm (1 cup) panko crumbs
- 75 gm (½ cup) cornflour
- 2 tsp onion powder

1 Combine rabbit, buttermilk and gochujang in a large bowl, mixing well, then cover and refrigerate overnight to marinate and tenderise the rabbit.

2 Heat oil in a deep-fryer or large saucepan to 170C. Combine crumb coating ingredients and 1 tsp freshly ground black pepper in a large bowl. Drain rabbit pieces and coat evenly in the crumb, shaking off excess. Deep-fry in batches, turning, until golden (4-5 minutes; hot oil will spit). Drain on paper towels, season to taste and serve hot with lemon cheeks.

NOTE Buttermilk is available from health-food shops. If it's unavailable, use yoghurt thinned with a little milk. Gochujang, Korean chilli paste, is available from Asian grocers; if it's unavailable substitute another chilli sauce.

WINE SUGGESTION A gamay rosé.

EASTER AT ESTER

EASTER AT ESTER

ROAST CARROTS WITH HONEY, SESAME AND PARMESAN

"Carrots and rabbit just go together," says Lindsay. "After all, rabbits eat carrots, so to serve them on the same table seems to bring together the circle of life in some strange way. This dish is a standard at Ester – I love the combination of simple flavours that come together to make it amazing."

PREP TIME 10 MINS, COOK 10 MINS
SERVES 6-8

—

- 2 bunches baby or heirloom carrots, scrubbed, patted dry
- 60 ml (¼ cup) olive oil
- 115 gm (⅓ cup) honey
- 2 tbsp tamari
- Sesame seeds, shaved Parmigiano-Reggiano and Lebanese cress (see note), to serve

1 Preheat oven to 250C or highest setting. Spread carrots in a roasting pan large enough to hold them snugly in a single layer, drizzle with oil and half the honey, season to taste and roast until liquid bubbles and carrots start to caramelise (6-8 minutes). Pour tamari and remaining honey over, toss to combine, season to taste with freshly ground black pepper and serve hot scattered with sesame seeds, Parmigiano-Reggiano and Lebanese cress.

NOTE Lebanese cress, which tastes like carrots, is available from select specialist greengrocers and farmers' markets. If you can't find it use flat-leaf parsley or the green carrot tops instead.

WINE SUGGESTION A dry German riesling.

BROCCOLINI WITH CHILLI AND
BURNT-GARLIC VINAIGRETTE

ROAST SPATCHCOCK WITH
GARLIC-BREAD SAUCE

EASTER AT ESTER

BROCCOLINI WITH CHILLI AND BURNT-GARLIC VINAIGRETTE

"Roasting broccolini brings out the best in it," says Lindsay. "When you boil it, it becomes quite sulphurous, but roasting it intensifies and deepens the flavours."

PREP TIME 10 MINS, COOK 10 MINS
SERVES 6-8

—

350 gm	(2 bunches) broccolini
100 ml	olive oil
8	garlic cloves, thickly sliced
2	long red chillies, finely chopped
60 ml	(¼ cup) sherry vinegar

1 Preheat oven to its highest setting. Toss broccolini in 1½ tbsp oil, then arrange in a roasting pan in a single layer, season to taste and roast until starting to brown (8-10 minutes).

2 Heat remaining oil in a frying pan over low heat, add garlic and fry, stirring occasionally, until dark golden (1-2 minutes). Remove with a slotted spoon and set aside. Add chilli to pan, cook until fragrant (1 minute), then remove from heat and add vinegar (take care, oil will spit). Add roast broccolini to pan, season to taste and serve hot scattered with crisp garlic.

ROAST SPATCHCOCK WITH GARLIC-BREAD SAUCE

"At Ester, it's all about the amazing wood-fired oven and there's nothing better than a simple roast chook," says Lindsay. "The garlic-bread sauce is my take on a classic and it puts to good use any of our day-old house-made sourdough." Start this recipe a day ahead to brine the bird.

PREP TIME 30 MINS, COOK 20 MINS (PLUS BRINING, RESTING)
SERVES 6-8

- 750 gm rock salt
- 2 spatchcock (500gm each)
- 2 lemons, halved

GARLIC-BREAD SAUCE
- 70 gm crustless sourdough bread, cut into 2cm cubes
- 250 gm unsalted butter, coarsely chopped
- 130 gm (about 15) garlic cloves, peeled
- 25 gm ($\frac{1}{4}$ cup) skim-milk powder
- 500 ml (2 cups) chicken stock

1 Stir salt and 1.5 litres water in a saucepan over medium heat to dissolve salt, then cool completely. Transfer to a non-reactive container (see cook's notes, p279), add spatchcock, cover and weight to submerge. Refrigerate overnight.

2 Preheat oven to 250C or highest setting. Drain spatchcock, pat dry with paper towels, then cut down each side of the backbone with a large knife or poultry scissors, remove backbone, flatten out bird and set aside.

3 Place lemon halves cut-sides down in a heavy roasting pan large enough to hold spatchcock in a single layer (or use 2 smaller roasting pans), place spatchcock on top skin-side up and season to taste. Roast until skin starts to char and juices run clear when thigh is pierced with a skewer (12-15 minutes). Set aside to rest in a warm place for 10 minutes.

4 For garlic-bread sauce, spread bread in a roasting pan and bake, stirring occasionally, until browned (4-5 minutes). Melt butter in a saucepan over medium-high heat, add garlic and cook until starting to soften (6-8 minutes). Add milk powder, cook until just golden brown (1-2 minutes), then stir in stock and bring to the boil. Add toasted bread and simmer until it breaks down and thickens the liquid (4-5 minutes). Reserve a few garlic cloves, then purée mixture with a hand-held blender until very smooth. Season to taste and keep warm.

5 To serve, cut spatchcock into pieces. Spoon garlic-bread sauce onto a serving plate, then place spatchcock pieces on top. Scatter with reserved garlic cloves, top with juice squeezed from the cooked lemons, which should be blackened, season to taste with pepper (you won't need any extra salt because of the brine) and serve hot.

WINE SUGGESTION A Greco di Tufo from Campania.

EASTER AT ESTER

BAKED APPLES WITH BURNT CREAM

"This is like the best apple crumble and cream you've ever had, only deconstructed," says Lindsay. *"It's a comforting dessert."* Begin this recipe a day ahead to set the cream; you'll also need a blowtorch.

PREP TIME 40 MINS, COOK 45 MINS (PLUS SETTING, COOLING)
SERVES 6-8

- 4 large Granny Smith apples, halved, cored
- Butter, for greasing
- 90 gm caster sugar
- Fried rosemary, to serve

BURNT CREAM
- 500 ml (2 cups) pouring cream
- Thinly peeled rind of 1 lemon
- 1 cinnamon quill
- 3 egg yolks
- 60 gm caster sugar, plus extra to serve

OLIVE-OIL CRUMB
- 150 gm (1 cup) plain flour
- 100 gm caster sugar
- 50 gm butter, coarsely chopped
- 50 ml olive oil

1 For burnt cream, bring cream, lemon rind and cinnamon quill to the boil in a saucepan over medium-high heat, then set aside to infuse and cool to room temperature (1 hour). Whisk yolks and sugar in a bowl until thick and pale (4-5 minutes), then strain in cream, whisking to combine. Return to pan over medium heat and stir continuously until mixture thickly coats the back of a wooden spoon (4-5 minutes). Pour into a 1-litre container and refrigerate overnight to set. When ready to serve, sprinkle an even layer of sugar on top and caramelise with a blowtorch.

2 For olive-oil crumb, preheat oven to 160C and line an oven tray with baking paper. Place ingredients in a bowl, rub together with your fingertips to a coarse crumb and season to taste with sea salt and white pepper. Spread in the prepared tray and bake, stirring occasionally, until golden (10-12 minutes). Cool, break into large pieces and store in an airtight container in the pantry for up to 5 days.

3 Preheat oven to 180C. Place apple halves cut-side down in a buttered baking dish large enough to fit them in a single layer. Stir sugar and 180ml water in a saucepan over medium-high heat to dissolve, bring to the boil, then pour syrup over apples. Bake uncovered, basting occasionally with syrup, until apples are tender and syrup starts to caramelise (20-25 minutes). Remove from the oven and cool.

4 Serve baked apples and burnt cream scattered with olive-oil crumb and fried rosemary.

WINE SUGGESTION A sweet chenin blanc.

SALTED-CARAMEL SEMIFREDDO

"This is super-simple but incredibly tasty," says Lindsay. "I could eat the black sesame mixture by the handful." Start this recipe a day ahead to give the semifreddo time to freeze.

PREP TIME 35 MINS, COOK 10 MINS (PLUS CHILLING, FREEZING)
SERVES 6-8

—

- 300 gm caster sugar
- 100 gm butter, diced
- 300 ml pouring cream
- 12 egg yolks
- 700 ml thickened cream, whisked to soft peaks

BLACK SESAME SUGAR
- 50 gm (2 tbsp) roasted black sesame seeds
- 2 tbsp caster sugar

1 Stir 200gm sugar and 100ml water in a saucepan over medium-high heat until sugar dissolves, then bring to the boil and cook until dark caramel (5-6 minutes). Add butter (be careful, hot caramel will spit) and swirl to combine. Stir in the cream, then add sea salt to taste (you'll need more than you think), and refrigerate to cool completely.

2 Whisk yolks and remaining sugar in a bowl over a saucepan of simmering water until thick and pale (6-7 minutes). Transfer to an electric mixer and whisk until cooled to room temperature. Fold in salted caramel, then thickened cream, transfer to a container and freeze overnight.

3 For black sesame sugar, process ingredients and 1 tbsp sea salt in a food processor to a sand-like texture. Store in an airtight container in the pantry for up to 2 weeks.

4 Serve scoops of semifreddo in chilled bowls, scattered with black sesame sugar.

WINE SUGGESTION A genmai-zake, a sake made with unpolished rice.

EASTER AT ESTER

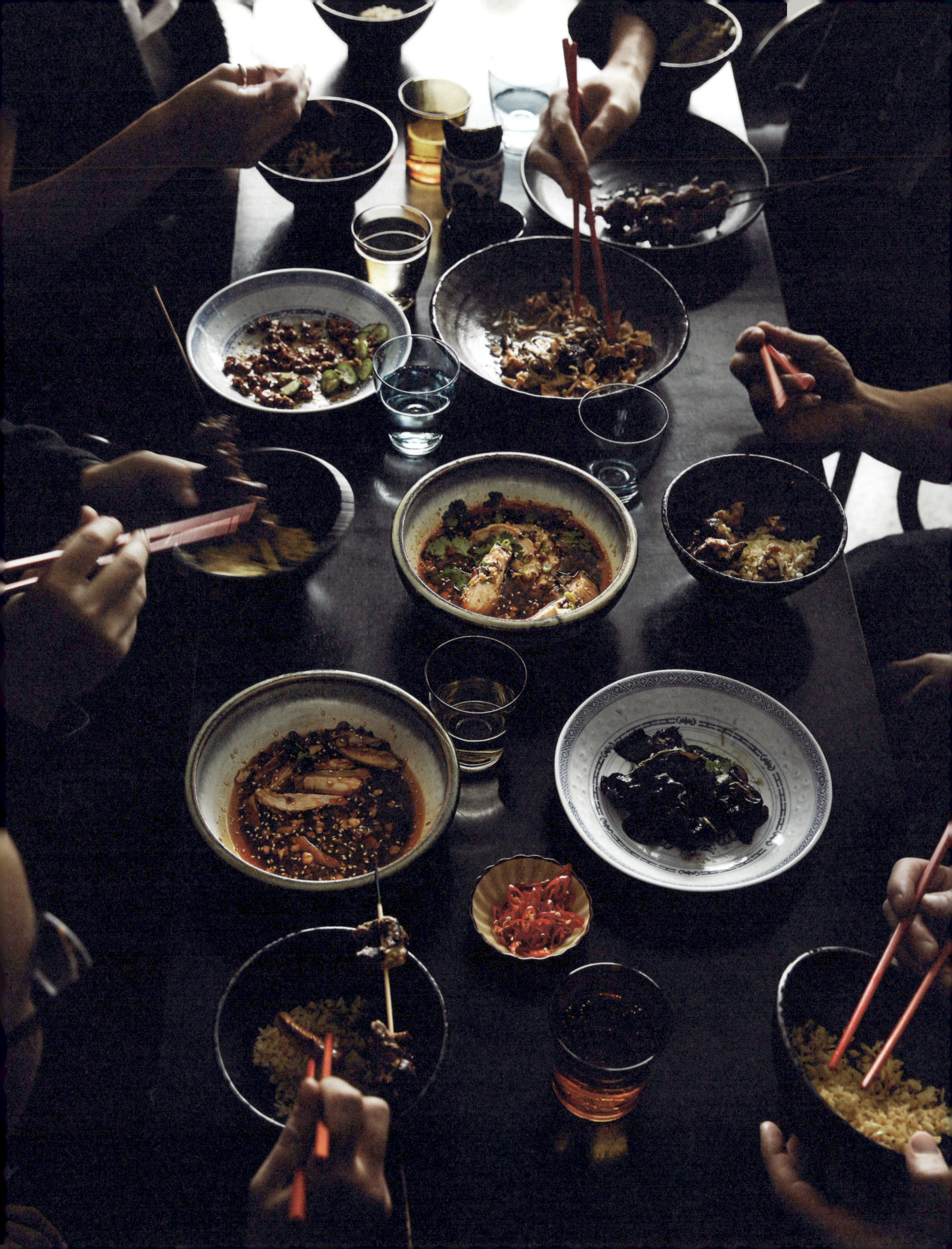

LEE HO FOOK'S ASIAN BANQUET

Chef Victor Liong has made a name for himself with modern riffs on Chinese classics, as this menu attests. Garlicky barbecued Xinjiang-style lamb skewers are just the beginning. The banquet is served.

—

+ Pickled black fungus

+ Chinese mushrooms with warrigal greens and Jerusalem artichokes

+ Xinjiang-style lamb skewers

+ Steamed barramundi, chilli black beans and pickled mustard greens

+ Fujian-style scallop and spanner crab fried rice

+ White-cut chicken, aromatic chilli oil and peanuts

+ Caramelised pineapple with green Sichuan peppercorn ice-cream

—

PICKLED BLACK FUNGUS

"Black fungus has a unique texture and also carries the flavour of a dressing really well," says Victor Liong. *"I like the idea of a textural, clean appetiser – it's my homage to old-school Chinese ingredients, but with a newer approach, serving it as a refreshing pickle."* Start this recipe a day ahead to marinate the fungus.

PREP TIME 15 MINS, COOK 2 MINS (PLUS MARINATING)
SERVES 4-6

—

- 1½ tbsp vegetable oil
- 200 gm black fungus, hard stems trimmed with scissors
- 30 ml Shaoxing wine
- 20 gm ginger, cut into julienne
- Coriander leaves, to serve

BLACK VINEGAR DRESSING
- 100 ml soy sauce
- 80 ml (⅓ cup) sugar syrup (see note)
- 60 ml (¼ cup) Chinkiang vinegar
- 1½ tbsp vegetable oil
- 1 tbsp sesame oil
- 1 tsp chilli oil (see note)
- 10 gm ginger, finely grated on a Microplane
- 1 small garlic clove, finely grated on a Microplane

1 Heat oil in a wok over high heat, add fungus and stir-fry for 1 minute. Add Shaoxing wine and stir-fry until liquid reduces (1 minute). Place in a colander to drain and cool to room temperature.

2 For black vinegar dressing, whisk ingredients and 100ml water in a non-reactive container (see cook's notes p279). Add fungus and ginger, and refrigerate overnight to marinate.

3 Place pickled black fungus in a serving bowl, drizzle with a little dressing, top with coriander and serve.

NOTE For sugar syrup, combine equal parts caster sugar and water, bring to the boil, then cool. Chilli oil is available from Asian supermarkets; Victor Liong prefers the Koon Yick Wah Kee brand.

DRINK SUGGESTIONS A fresh crisp viognier, or a lager.

LEE HO FOOK'S ASIAN BANQUET

LEE HO FOOK'S ASIAN BANQUET

CHINESE MUSHROOMS WITH WARRIGAL GREENS AND JERUSALEM ARTICHOKES

"I like the earthy tones of the mushrooms, the leafy aesthetics of the Jerusalem artichokes, the meaty texture of the warrigal greens," says Liong. "It's a wonderful vegetable stir-fry."

PREP TIME 20 MINS, COOK 20 MINS
SERVES 4-6

—

100 gm each shimeji and oyster mushrooms, cut into bite-sized pieces
100 gm shiitake mushrooms, stems trimmed, mushrooms halved
50 gm enoki mushrooms, cut into 2cm batons
30 gm warrigal greens, leaves only (see note)
2¾ tsp (10gm) tapioca starch, dissolved in 1 tbsp cold water

MUSHROOM STOCK
1 tsp vegetable oil
½ onion, thinly sliced
1 spring onion (green part only), chopped
1 tbsp thinly sliced ginger
2 coriander stems
1 large garlic clove, bruised
6 gm (2 tbsp) dried porcini mushrooms
1¼ tbsp white soy sauce (see note)
¾ tsp caster sugar
½ tsp chicken stock powder, such as Knorr (see note)

JERUSALEM ARTICHOKE CHIPS
Vegetable oil, for frying
150 gm (2 large) Jerusalem artichokes, washed and very thinly sliced on a mandolin

1 For mushroom stock, heat oil in a frying pan over medium-high heat, add onion, spring onion, ginger, coriander stems and garlic, and sauté until golden (6-8 minutes). Place dried porcini in a large saucepan with 800ml water and bring to the boil. Add onion mixture, bring back to the boil, then simmer over low heat to develop flavours (20 minutes). Strain and stir in remaining ingredients and ½ tsp salt.

2 For artichoke chips, heat 5cm oil in a deep saucepan to 175C and fry artichoke slices in batches, stirring constantly, until crisp and golden brown (2-4 minutes; be careful, hot oil will spit). Drain on paper towels.

3 Top up oil to about 8cm deep and heat to 180C. Deep-fry shimeji, oyster and shiitake mushrooms in batches until golden brown (1-2 minutes), then drain in a colander.

4 Bring mushroom stock to the boil, add fried mushrooms and simmer for mushrooms to absorb stock (1-2 minutes). Add enoki and warrigal greens, and stir-fry until greens just wilt (10-20 seconds). Slowly add tapioca starch, stirring until a shiny, thickened sauce forms (1-2 minutes). Add a good pinch of ground white pepper and serve topped with Jerusalem artichoke chips.

NOTE Warrigal greens are available from select greengrocers. To find your local supplier, go to outbackpride.com.au and see "distributors"; if they're unavailable, substitute spinach. White soy sauce, or shiro shoyu, is available from Japanese grocers such as Tokyo Mart and Chef's Armoury; if it's unavailable, substitute regular soy sauce. Knorr chicken stock powder is available at Asian supermarkets.

WINE SUGGESTION A shiraz.

XINJIANG-STYLE LAMB SKEWERS

"These skewers are great as a snack or for your next barbecue," says Liong.

PREP TIME 20 MINS, COOK 10 MINS (PLUS MARINATING)
SERVES 4-6

- 5 garlic cloves, coarsely chopped
- 75 ml Shaoxing wine
- 35 ml liquid seasoning, such as Knorr (see note)
- 200 gm fermented tofu (see note)
- 150 gm sweet bean paste (see note)
- 1½ tsp (7gm) bicarbonate of soda
- 500 gm piece of lamb shoulder, sliced across the grain
- 20 bamboo skewers, soaked in water for at least 1 hour

SPICE SEASONING
- 1¾ tsp cumin seeds
- 1 tsp Sichuan peppercorns
- 1 tsp fennel seeds
- ¾ tsp sumac
- ¾ tsp shichimi togarashi (see note)

VINEGAR SEASONING
- 50 ml Chinkiang vinegar
- 1 tbsp soy sauce

1 Process garlic, Shaoxing and liquid seasoning in a blender. Add fermented tofu and sweet bean paste, blend until smooth, then add bicarbonate of soda. Place lamb in a non-reactive bowl (see cook's notes p279), pour in marinade, mix to coat, then refrigerate for at least 1 hour to marinate. Brush excess marinade from lamb, then thread lamb onto skewers and refrigerate.

2 For spice seasoning, coarsely grind cumin, Sichuan peppercorns and fennel seeds in a spice grinder or with a mortar and pestle. Add 1 tsp sea salt and pulse lightly or crush, then add sumac and shichimi togarashi. Store in an airtight container.

3 For vinegar seasoning, combine ingredients in a spray bottle.

4 Grill lamb skewers on a barbecue or in a char-grill pan over medium-high heat, turning and spraying occasionally with vinegar seasoning, until charred and just cooked (2-3 minutes each side), sprinkling with dry spice mix in the last minute of cooking. Serve scattered with extra spice seasoning.

NOTE Knorr liquid seasoning, fermented tofu, sweet bean paste, also known as tian mian jiang (Victor Liong prefers to use Fu Chi brand), and shichimi togarashi, a Japanese spice blend, are available from Asian supermarkets and Chinese grocers.

WINE SUGGESTION A sparkling shiraz.

LEE HO FOOK'S ASIAN BANQUET

LEE HO FOOK'S ASIAN BANQUET

STEAMED BARRAMUNDI, CHILLI BLACK BEANS AND PICKLED MUSTARD GREENS

"I like the lightness of steamed fish," says Liong. "Barramundi lends itself perfectly to steaming – it's so juicy and tender, and pairs well with heavier winter flavours such as pickles and preserved vegetables. I also like the savoury acidity that mustard greens add to this dish." Start this recipe three days ahead to make the ginger oil and salted chilli.

PREP TIME 30 MINS, COOK 35 MINS (PLUS INFUSING)
SERVES 4-6

—

- 400 gm piece of barramundi, skin on and cut into 50gm pieces
- 60 gm pickled mustard greens, thinly sliced (see note)
- 20 gm ginger, peeled, cut into julienne
- 30 ml Shaoxing wine
- 2 spring onions, very thinly sliced
- 1 cup each (loosely packed) coriander and Thai basil

GINGER OIL
- 100 ml vegetable oil
- 50 gm ginger, skin on, washed and chopped

SALTED CHILLI
- 30 gm long red chillies, chopped
- 4 garlic cloves
- 10 gm peeled ginger, chopped

CHILLI BLACK BEAN PASTE
- 3 tsp chilli crisp sauce (Lao Gan Ma brand)
- 2 tsp chopped fermented salted black beans (see note)
- 1 tsp white vinegar
- ½ tsp caster sugar

WHITE SOY DRESSING
- 1 tsp rice wine vinegar
- 1 tsp caster sugar
- 1½ tbsp soy sauce
- 1¾ tbsp white soy sauce (see note)

1 For ginger oil, process oil and ginger in a blender until smooth, then transfer to a saucepan and bring to the boil. Reduce heat to low and simmer, stirring and scraping base of pan often to prevent catching, until oil is fragrant (15-20 minutes). Cool to room temperature, then refrigerate in an airtight container for 3 days to infuse. Strain into a bowl through muslin or a fine strainer. This recipe makes more than you need here, but it will keep refrigerated in an airtight container for a month.

2 For salted chilli, process ingredients in a small food processor with a generous teaspoonful (6gm) of fine salt until finely chopped, then transfer to a container with a lid, cover and stand at room temperature overnight to ferment. Refrigerate in an airtight container until required.

3 For chilli black bean paste, combine ingredients and salted chilli in a bowl, then refrigerate overnight for flavours to develop.

4 For white soy dressing, whisk ingredients and 50ml water in a bowl and set aside.

5 Place barramundi on a large plate that fits inside a large steamer. Cover generously with chilli black bean paste, top with mustard greens and ginger, pour Shaoxing over and steam over high heat, until a skewer pierces the flesh easily (10-12 minutes).

6 To serve, transfer fish to a serving dish, pour white soy dressing over, top with spring onion, coriander and Thai basil, and drizzle with ginger oil to taste.

NOTE Pickled mustard greens and fermented salted black beans are available from Asian supermarkets. White soy sauce, or shiro shoyu, is available from Japanese grocers such as Tokyo Mart and Chef's Armoury; if it's unavailable, substitute regular soy sauce.

WINE SUGGESTION A savoury pinot noir.

FUJIAN-STYLE SCALLOP AND SPANNER CRAB FRIED RICE (FAR LEFT)

FUJIAN-STYLE SCALLOP AND SPANNER CRAB FRIED RICE

"This is a classic dish that has it all," says Liong. "There's heat and depth from the XO sauce, a comforting, rich scallop and spanner crab sauce and egg fried rice – a winter classic, often poorly executed." Start this recipe at least half a day ahead to dry the rice.

PREP TIME 20 MINS, COOK 45 MINS (PLUS DRYING)
SERVES 4-6

—

- 250 gm jasmine rice, rinsed and drained at least 3 times to remove excess starch
- 80 ml (⅓ cup) vegetable oil
- 2 eggs plus 1 egg yolk, whisked
- 1 tsp caster sugar
- 1 tsp chicken stock powder, such as Knorr (see note)
- ½ tsp ground white pepper
- 1 tbsp XO sauce
- 2 spring onions, thinly sliced

FUJIAN SEAFOOD SAUCE
- 350 ml chicken stock
- 70 ml white soy sauce (see note)
- 2 tsp caster sugar
- 1 tsp ginger oil (see recipe p163), or ¼ tsp finely grated ginger
- 1 tsp sesame oil
- 1½ eggwhites (50gm)
- 80 gm spanner crab meat
- 80 gm scallops, cut into small pieces
- 30 gm tapioca starch, dissolved in 50ml cold water

1 Place rice and 480ml water in a saucepan with a tight-fitting lid and bring to the boil, stirring once, then cover, reduce heat to very low and cook for 12 minutes. Turn off heat, don't uncover and leave on residual heat for 20 minutes to finish cooking. Uncover, fluff up rice with a fork, then spread rice evenly on a tray and leave to cool, fanning occasionally to speed the process. Refrigerate uncovered to dry completely (3-4 hours).
2 For Fujian seafood sauce, place stock in a saucepan, bring to the boil, then add white soy sauce, sugar, oils and ¼ tsp salt. Return to the boil and whisk in eggwhites to scramble (30-40 seconds), then add seafood and simmer until just cooked (1-2 minutes). Add tapioca starch and stir until sauce thickly coats the back of a spoon (1-2 minutes). Keep warm.
3 Heat vegetable oil in a wok over high heat until smoking, add eggs and stir until scrambled (1 minute). Add rice and stir-fry, breaking it up as you go, until hot (2-3 minutes), then add sugar, chicken stock powder and pepper, and stir to coat rice. Add XO sauce and spring onion, season to taste, transfer to a serving bowl, pour Fujian sauce on top and serve.
NOTE Knorr chicken stock powder is available at Asian supermarkets. White soy sauce, or shiro shoyu, is available from Japanese grocers such as Tokyo Mart and Chef's Armoury; if it's unavailable, substitute regular soy sauce.
WINE SUGGESTIONS A white Burgundy or other rich chardonnay.

VICTOR LIONG

LEE HO FOOK'S ASIAN BANQUET

LEE HO FOOK'S ASIAN BANQUET

WHITE-CUT CHICKEN, AROMATIC CHILLI OIL AND PEANUTS

"White-cut chicken, in my opinion, is one of the great Chinese techniques," says Liong. "It preserves the succulence of the meat and showcases its silky texture. We've made it with a complex yet light dressing to add interest to a classic technique." Start this recipe a day ahead to make the salted chilli (see recipe p163).

PREP TIME 30 MINS, COOK 50 MINS (PLUS COOLING, CHILLING)
SERVES 4-6

- 650 ml Shaoxing wine
- 80 gm fine salt
- 20 gm ginger, unpeeled and thinly sliced
- 1 large spring onion, coarsely chopped
- 4 chicken Marylands (about 350gm each)
- 200 ml vegetable oil
- 1½ tbsp Sichuan peppercorns
- 1 quantity salted chilli (see recipe p163)
- 100 gm chillies in oil (Lao Gan Ma brand)
- 60 ml (¼ cup) chilli oil (see note)
- Finely chopped spring onions, sesame seeds and coriander leaves, to serve
- 1 lemon

CRISP PEANUTS
- 30 gm raw peeled peanuts
- Vegetable oil, for frying

SOY DRESSING
- 125 ml (½ cup) soy sauce
- 60 ml (¼ cup) Chinkiang vinegar
- 60 ml (¼ cup) mirin
- 2 tbsp rice wine vinegar
- 1¼ tbsp sugar syrup (see note)
- 1 small garlic clove, finely grated on a Microplane
- 5 gm ginger, finely grated on a Microplane

1 Bring Shaoxing, salt, ginger, spring onion and 4 litres water to the boil in a large saucepan or stockpot with a tight-fitting lid. Add chicken, bring back to the boil, cover, then turn off heat and leave chicken to cook until juices run clear when a skewer is inserted at the joint and the internal temperature is 70C on a meat thermometer (40-45 minutes). Remove chicken from stock, cool to room temperature, then refrigerate until chilled (2-3 hours). Cut chicken at intervals through the bone and refrigerate until required.

2 Meanwhile, for crisp peanuts, mix 2 tsp salt with 500ml water in a saucepan, add peanuts, bring to the boil, then reduce heat to medium and simmer until peanuts are al dente (20-25 minutes). Drain well in a colander. Heat 5cm oil in a wok over high heat until it shimmers. Add peanuts and fry, stirring continuously, until golden brown (2 minutes). Drain on paper towels, cool and chop before using. Peanuts will keep stored in an airtight container for 4 weeks.

3 For soy dressing, whisk ingredients in a bowl. Dressing will keep refrigerated in an airtight container for 2 weeks.

4 Heat vegetable oil and Sichuan peppercorns in a wok over low-medium heat until peppercorns float and start to turn a lighter shade of red (1-2 minutes). Add salted chilli and cook until most of the moisture is cooked out and oil is aromatic (3-4 minutes). Add chillies in oil and cook until paste is uniform in colour (1-2 minutes). Remove from heat, add chilli oil and cool completely.

5 To serve, place sliced chicken in a deep serving dish, pour soy dressing over, then salted chilli oil to taste (remaining oil will keep refrigerated in an airtight container for up to a month), scatter with peanuts, spring onion, sesame seeds and coriander, and finely grate lemon rind over the top.

NOTE Chilli oil is available from Asian supermarkets; Victor Liong prefers the Koon Yick Wah Kee brand. For sugar syrup, combine equal parts caster sugar and water, bring to the boil, then cool.

WINE SUGGESTION A German-style aromatic riesling with a bit of sweetness.

CARAMELISED PINEAPPLE WITH GREEN SICHUAN PEPPERCORN ICE-CREAM

"This combination was first introduced to me by Mark Best of Sydney's Marque restaurant when I was a chef de partie there," says Liong. "I loved it so much I stole it. Thanks, Besty."

PREP TIME 15 MINS, COOK 45 MINS (PLUS FREEZING, COOLING)
SERVES 4-6

—

600 gm caster sugar
300 gm pineapple, cut into 8mm dice

GREEN SICHUAN PEPPERCORN ICE-CREAM

20 gm green Sichuan peppercorns (see note)
1.2 litres milk
300 ml pouring cream
12 egg yolks
200 gm caster sugar

1 For green Sichuan peppercorn ice-cream, preheat oven to 160C and roast peppercorns on a tray, stirring occasionally, until aromatic (10-15 minutes). Place in a saucepan with milk and cream and bring to the boil. Meanwhile, whisk egg yolks and sugar in a bowl until light and fluffy, then, whisking continuously, pour in hot milk mixture. Return to the pan and stir continuously over low heat until mixture reaches 85C on a sugar thermometer or thickly coats the back of a spoon (15-20 minutes). Pour into a bowl placed over a bowl filled with ice to cool, then strain mixture through a sieve (discard peppercorns). Churn in an ice-cream machine, then freeze in an airtight container (around 3 hours). Makes 2 litres.

2 Bring sugar and 200ml water to the boil in a saucepan over high heat, stirring until sugar dissolves, then boil without stirring, but swirling the pan occasionally, until a dark caramel forms or it reaches 160C on a sugar thermometer (10-12 minutes). Remove from heat, slowly add pineapple pieces (be careful, hot caramel will spit) and stir to coat with caramel, then return pan to heat and bring back to the boil. Cool to room temperature (about 1 hour), then strain caramel into a bowl, refrigerate pineapple in a container to chill and reserve caramel at room temperature.

3 To serve, spoon a little caramelised pineapple into serving bowls, top with a generous scoop of ice-cream and drizzle with caramel.

NOTE Green Sichuan peppercorns are available from Asian supermarkets.
DRINK SUGGESTION Jasmine tea.

LEE HO FOOK'S ASIAN BANQUET

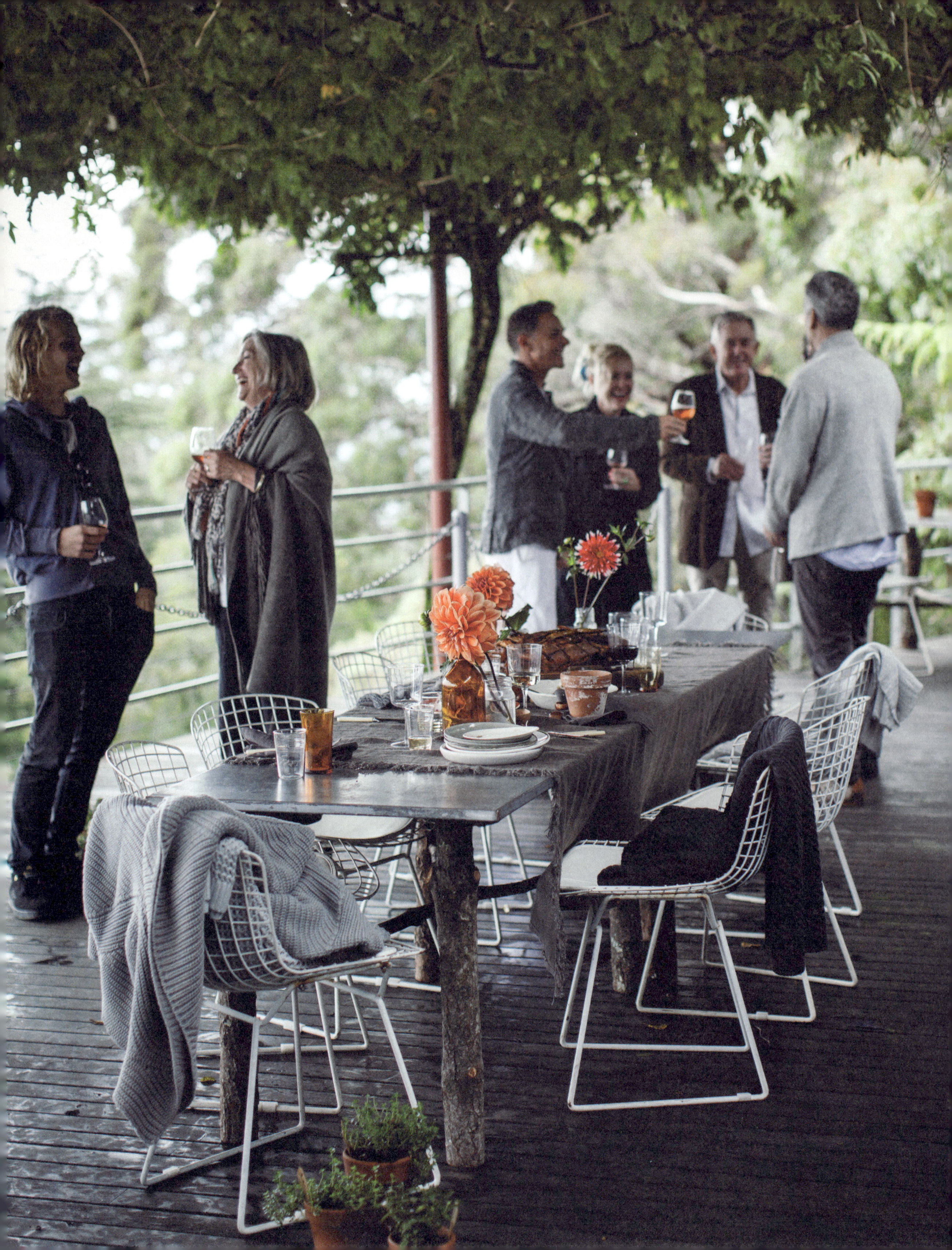

BLUE MOUNTAINS
HARVEST LUNCH

You'll want to gather a crowd for this hearty menu designed for long winter lunching by Sydney chef Sean Moran. Moran describes the food as soulful and when you take your first forkful of the slow-cooked pork shoulder with fennel you'll understand why.

—

+ Celeriac and Gruyère fritters

+ Rabbit broth with rabbit and barley dumplings

+ Dill-cured rainbow trout with beetroot and potato cakes and fresh horseradish

+ Chestnut "worms" with all sorts of mushrooms

+ Slow-roasted pork shoulder with fennel

+ Winter slaw

+ Parsnip puddings

—

CELERIAC AND GRUYÈRE FRITTERS

"My other name for these little winter warmers is celeriac and Gruyère delights because they're exactly that – the combination of earthy celery flavour with melting Gruyère and a zap of zest is really spot on," says Sean Moran. "They're great scattered over a leaf salad or as part of an antipasto plate, yet even better served alone as an appetiser, with a little local fizz."

PREP TIME 20 MINS, COOK 30 MINS (PLUS CHILLING)
MAKES 18

—

Juice and finely grated rind of 1 lemon
50 gm ($\frac{1}{3}$ cup) plain flour
1 tbsp salt
1 thyme sprig
1 celeriac (600gm), peeled and quartered
50 gm Gruyère (preferably Heidi Farm), cut into 5mm dice
1 garlic clove, finely chopped
1 egg, lightly beaten
$\frac{3}{4}$ cup finely chopped flat-leaf parsley
100 ml vegetable or canola oil

1 Whisk lemon juice, half the flour and the salt into 1 litre of water in a saucepan. Add thyme and bring to the boil, then add celeriac and boil until tender (15 minutes). Drain and cool, then grate celeriac into a bowl, add remaining flour, lemon rind, Gruyère, garlic, egg and parsley, and season to taste. Mix well by hand, then form into 18 small balls, place on a tray lined with baking paper and refrigerate for at least 30 minutes.
2 Heat oil in a large frying pan over medium heat. Carefully add balls in batches and fry, turning occasionally, until golden and crisp (7-9 minutes). Transfer fritters to paper towels with a slotted spoon, season and serve hot.
DRINK SUGGESTION Apple cider.

BLUE MOUNTAINS HARVEST LUNCH

BLUE MOUNTAINS HARVEST LUNCH

RABBIT BROTH WITH RABBIT AND BARLEY DUMPLINGS

"This is a full-flavoured broth with daintily wrapped rabbit dumplings for those of us with time on our hands and friends we really love," says Moran.

PREP TIME 1 HR, COOK 3 HRS 40 MINS
SERVES 10-12

—

- 1 rabbit (1.5kg; you may need to order it ahead)
- 100 ml olive oil
- 3 large onions, thinly sliced
- 3 large carrots, thinly sliced
- 3 celery stalks, thinly sliced
- 1 garlic head, 3 cloves finely chopped, remainder coarsely chopped
- 250 ml dry white wine
- 4 litres chicken stock
- 1 tsp juniper berries, crushed
- 6 peppercorns
- 1 fresh bay leaf
- 100 gm pearl barley
- 2 eggwhites, plus 1 extra, lightly whisked, for brushing
- 300 ml pouring cream
- ¼ cup French tarragon, finely chopped
- ¼ cup finely chopped chives
- Finely grated rind of 1 orange
- 24 cavolo nero leaves (about 2 bunches)

1 Pull kidneys and liver from rabbit carcass then, using a sharp boning knife, debone rear legs, loins and fillets off saddle (don't bother scraping meat off the thinner front legs – these can be poached in the stock and served separately alongside the broth). Reserve bones.

2 Heat oil in a large wide saucepan, add rabbit bones, onion, carrot, celery and coarsely chopped garlic, and cook over high heat, stirring as needed, until golden (20-30 minutes). Deglaze pan with wine, then add stock, juniper berries, peppercorns and bay leaf, and bring to the boil. Reduce heat to low, add front legs of rabbit and simmer until meat is completely tender (30-40 minutes). Remove legs from pan and keep warm. Continue simmering stock for 1½ hours until well flavoured, then strain and keep warm.

3 Dry-roast barley in a small saucepan over medium heat until golden and nuttily fragrant (4-6 minutes). Add 500ml stock, bring to the boil, then reduce heat to low, cover and simmer until tender and stock has been absorbed (45 minutes to 1 hour). Pour barley onto a wide plate to cool.

4 Dice rabbit loin and fillet into 5mm pieces and set aside. Cut rear leg meat into rough 2cm chunks and process in a food processor until finely chopped, then add eggwhites and 1 tsp salt, and process to a purée. Transfer to a bowl, add cooked barley, finely chopped garlic, cream, tarragon, chives, orange rind and diced loin and fillet meat, season with freshly cracked black pepper, then beat well with a wooden spoon to incorporate. Test mix for seasoning by poaching a small teaspoonful in simmering stock.

5 Blanch cavolo nero in a saucepan of salted water (2-3 minutes; see cook's notes p279), then refresh in cold water. Drain and pat leaves dry with paper towels, then cut away central stalk so you are left with 2 pieces from each leaf. Brush each piece with eggwhite, then place a small tablespoonful of rabbit mixture on top and roll into a parcel. Set aside on a tray in the refrigerator and repeat with remaining leaves and rabbit mixture.

6 Bring remaining stock to a simmer over medium-high heat, season to taste, then add dumplings in batches and poach until cooked (2-3 minutes; scrape together the last of the mix for a tester and cut in half to check). Divide among warmed bowls. Strain broth again, ladle into bowls and serve, with the addition of the tender front legs for two favourite guests.

WINE SUGGESTION A pinot gris.

SEAN MORAN

BLUE MOUNTAINS HARVEST LUNCH

DILL-CURED RAINBOW TROUT WITH BEETROOT AND POTATO CAKES AND FRESH HORSERADISH

"Dill-cured trout served with potato cakes and horseradish cream may be somewhat traditional to some and a luxury to others like me," Moran says. "With a tweak of grated beetroot and onion bleeding richer hues and, oomph, may the luxury live on." Start this recipe a day ahead to cure the trout.

PREP TIME 30 MINS, COOK 20 MINS (PLUS CURING)
SERVES 10

—

- 1 cup (loosely packed) fresh dill
- Finely grated rind of 1 orange
- 1 garlic clove, coarsely chopped
- 1 tsp juniper berries
- 110 gm (½ cup) caster sugar
- 145 gm (½ cup) coarse salt
- 1 rainbow trout (around 1kg), filleted, skin on, pin boned
- Crème fraîche, finely grated horseradish root and radish sprouts, to serve

BEETROOT AND POTATO CAKES

- 1 kg Desiree potatoes (about 3 large), peeled, halved
- 1 beetroot, peeled, coarsely grated
- 1 onion, coarsely grated
- Handful thyme, finely chopped
- 250 gm duck fat or canola oil

1 Pound dill, orange rind, garlic and juniper berries with a mortar and pestle to a coarse paste, then add sugar and salt, and mix well. Rub mixture generously all over trout fillets, then place in a non-reactive container (see cook's notes p279) and refrigerate overnight to cure.

2 For beetroot and potato cakes, place potatoes in a saucepan with a generous pinch of salt, cover with cold water, and bring to the boil over medium heat. Drain immediately and, when cool enough to handle, coarsely grate potatoes into a bowl. Add beetroot, onion and thyme, season to taste and mix well. Form mixture into 10 round, flat patties, roughly 75gm each, pressing firmly together, and set aside on a tray.

3 Shake cure mix off trout fillets and pat dry with paper towels, then remove skin and thinly slice trout with a sharp filleting knife.

4 Heat duck fat or oil in a large frying pan and shallow-fry patties in batches, turning occasionally, until golden and crisp on each side (5-6 minutes), then drain on paper towels. Serve hot with sliced trout, topped with crème fraîche, and scattered with finely grated horseradish and radish sprouts.

WINE SUGGESTION A shiraz rosé.

BLUE MOUNTAINS HARVEST LUNCH

WINTER SLAW

CHESTNUT "WORMS" WITH ALL
SORTS OF MUSHROOMS

SLOW-ROASTED PORK SHOULDER
WITH FENNEL

180 GOURMET TRAVELLER | MENUS

BLUE MOUNTAINS HARVEST LUNCH

CHESTNUT "WORMS" WITH ALL SORTS OF MUSHROOMS

"If, like me, you find comfort in the sweet, earthy mealiness of chestnuts, then this is your dish," says Moran. "These worms are right at home wriggling among all sorts of mushrooms. The potato skins left over from this recipe can be deep-fried for great snacks, or crumbled and scattered over this dish for added crunch."

PREP TIME 2 HRS, COOK 45 MINS
SERVES 10

—

- 500 gm chestnuts
- 250 ml milk
- 1 kg Nicola potatoes (about 16), scrubbed
- 1 handful coarse salt
- 250 gm plain flour, plus extra for rolling
- 1 large egg (70gm), lightly whisked
- Finely grated nutmeg, to taste
- 160 ml olive oil
- 1 kg various mushrooms, such as pine, slippery jack, king brown, Swiss brown or field, thinly sliced, or shimeji, broken into clumps
- 4 garlic cloves, finely chopped
- 200 ml chicken or vegetable stock
- 1 handful (2 cups) rocket, coarsely sliced
- Finely grated aged goat's cheese or parmesan, to serve

1 Preheat oven to 200C. Make a small slit in each chestnut using a sharp knife and roast until slightly split (20 minutes). Peel using a small sharp knife while still hot (wear rubber gloves), place chestnut meat in a saucepan with milk, bring to a gentle simmer and cook, covered, until all the milk has evaporated (around 20 minutes).

2 Meanwhile, prick potatoes all over with a fork. Scatter salt over a large oven tray, place potatoes on top and bake until tender when tested with a skewer (about 1 hour). Cut potatoes in half, scoop out the flesh and, in batches, push through a potato ricer along with chestnut meat onto a clean work bench.

3 Scatter flour evenly over potato and chestnut mixture, drizzle egg over, add nutmeg and salt to taste, then bring dough together using a pastry scraper, chopping and scraping to combine (avoid kneading dough). Form into a ball and wrap in a damp cloth. Cut off a piece of dough, flour your hands, then roll dough on a lightly floured surface into a pencil-thick length and cut into pieces 10cm-15cm long. Transfer to a lightly floured tray, cover with a damp cloth and repeat with remaining dough.

4 Heat 100ml oil in a frying pan, add a third of the mushrooms, season to taste and sauté until caramelised (8-10 minutes). Transfer to a large plate and keep warm. Repeat with remaining mushrooms, then wipe pan clean and return to heat with remaining oil.

5 Cook chestnut worms in a saucepan of boiling salted water until they rise to the surface (1-2 minutes). Drain, add to frying pan and cook, swirling occasionally, until lightly caramelised (7 minutes), adding garlic during the last minute of cooking. Deglaze pan with stock, bring to the boil, add mushrooms and all their juices, rocket and cheese, toss together and serve.
WINE SUGGESTION Pinot noir.

SLOW-ROASTED PORK SHOULDER WITH FENNEL

"Everyone loves a full-flavoured, meltingly tender shoulder of pork, even the cook," says Moran. *"It's easy to prepare, it wows at the table and those seductive anise wafts – a thrill to wake up to."*

PREP TIME 15 MINS, COOK 8½ HOURS
SERVES 8-10

—

- 1 bone-in pork shoulder (5kg-6kg)
- 1 head garlic, cloves peeled
- 1 tbsp fennel seeds
- 10 large fennel bulbs, halved
- 750 ml white wine
- 75 ml apple cider vinegar

1 Preheat oven to 200C. Carefully score skin of pork in a 2.5cm diamond pattern just deep enough to penetrate fat but not flesh. Pound garlic, fennel seeds and 2 heaped tsp salt to a paste with a mortar and pestle. Rub mixture all over pork, pushing into scored skin, then place skin-side up in a large deep roasting pan. Place fennel bulbs neatly around pork and pour in wine. Reduce oven to 100C and roast pork overnight (or for at least 8 hours). Remove shoulder and fennel from pan and set aside covered 20 minutes to rest.

2 Meanwhile, add vinegar to pan and simmer cooking liquid to reduce to a sauce consistency (25-30 minutes). Keep warm.

3 Slice pork and serve with sauce and winter slaw.

WINE SUGGESTION Sangiovese.

WINTER SLAW

PREP TIME 10 MINS
SERVES 8-10

—

- ⅓ cup pepitas
- 350 gm (¼ head) each red cabbage and white cabbage, thinly sliced
- 2 bulbs (350gm each) kohlrabi, unpeeled, thinly sliced
- 2 red carrots, cut into thin ribbons with a vegetable peeler
- 6 golden shallots, thinly sliced
- 4 Granny Smith apples, cored, quartered, thinly sliced
- 1 radish, thinly sliced on a mandolin
- 75 ml apple cider vinegar
- 100 ml extra-virgin olive oil

1 Dry-roast pepitas in a small frying pan over medium-high heat (1-2 minutes). Set aside to cool.

2 Combine remaining ingredients in a large bowl, season to taste, add pepitas and toss well. Stand for a few minutes before serving with pork.

BLUE MOUNTAINS HARVEST LUNCH

PARSNIP PUDDINGS

"I know what you're thinking – parsnip puddings?" says Moran. "I understand completely; however, much like carrots in a cake or pumpkin in a pie, parsnips have surprisingly sweet flesh and even more so after the first winter frost. As a bonus, the starch in parsnips gives these wintry puds a unique richness all their own."

PREP TIME 30 MINS, COOK 45 MINS
MAKES 10

---

800 gm parsnips (about 4), trimmed, peeled, cored and cut into large even chunks
250 gm unsalted softened butter, plus extra for greasing moulds
50 ml treacle
400 gm candied ginger, 100gm coarsely chopped, remainder cut into 30 thin slices
250 gm brown sugar
70 gm ($\frac{1}{2}$ cup) currants steeped in 60ml brandy
140 gm (2 cups) coarse dry breadcrumbs
$\frac{1}{2}$ tsp finely grated nutmeg
$\frac{1}{2}$ tsp ground cinnamon
$\frac{1}{2}$ tsp ground cloves
$\frac{1}{2}$ tsp baking powder
2 large eggs, lightly whisked
125 ml ($\frac{1}{2}$ cup) buttermilk

POURING CUSTARD

600 ml pouring cream
600 ml milk
1 vanilla bean, split, seeds scraped
12 egg yolks
165 gm ($\frac{3}{4}$ cup) caster sugar

1 Steam parsnips over a saucepan of simmering water until tender when tested with a skewer (15-20 minutes). Cool to room temperature (30-45 minutes), then coarsely grate. Reserve.
2 Butter ten 125ml metal dariole moulds with extra butter, then place a teaspoonful of treacle in each and arrange 3 slices of candied ginger in the base of each.
3 Beat butter and sugar in an electric mixer until pale and fluffy (4-5 minutes). Meanwhile, combine chopped ginger, currants and brandy, breadcrumbs, spices, baking powder and ½ tsp salt in a bowl. Gradually beat eggs into butter mixture, then add buttermilk and combine well. Gently fold in grated parsnip and ginger mixture with a large spatula. Divide batter among dariole moulds, filling to 1cm below rims, smooth tops, cover with foil, tie with string and steam in a steamer over simmering water until cooked through when tested with a skewer (30-40 minutes).
4 For pouring custard, bring cream, milk and vanilla bean and seeds to the boil in a saucepan over high heat. Whisk yolks and sugar in a bowl, then, whisking continuously, add milk mixture. Return to pan, reduce heat to low and cook, stirring continuously with a wooden spoon in a figure-of-eight pattern to prevent the custard catching, until thick enough to coat the spoon and just starting to coagulate at the bottom when you tilt the pan (3-4 minutes). Swiftly pour custard through a fine strainer into a bowl placed over ice, stirring for a few seconds to cool slightly. If not using straight away, gently reheat custard in a stainless steel saucepan over low heat, whisking continuously, until warmed through (avoid boiling).
5 To serve, carefully remove puddings from steamer, run a small knife around the inside of each mould, then invert onto plates and serve with custard.
WINE SUGGESTION A sticky dessert gewürztraminer.

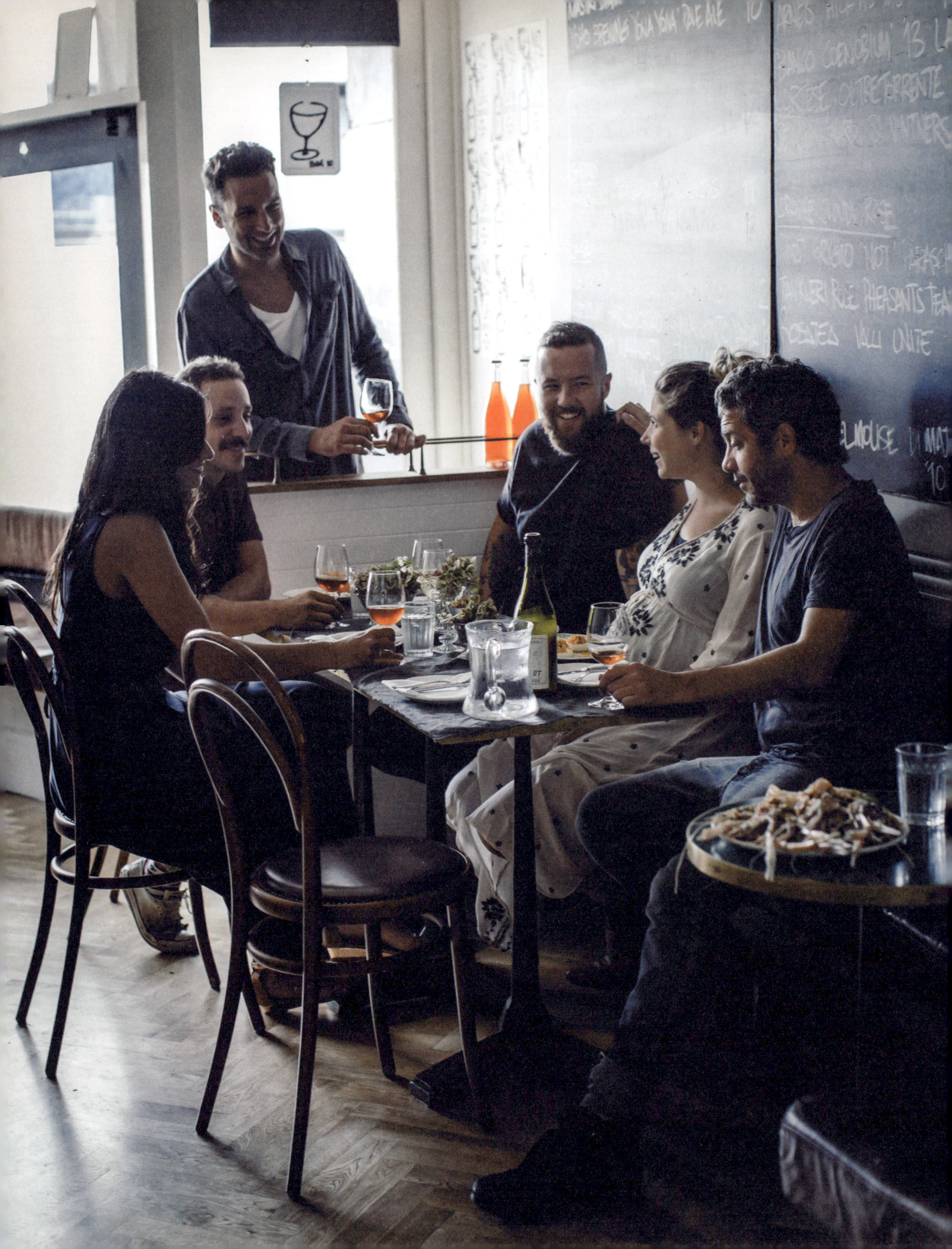

EASTER AT 10 WILLIAM ST

Long weekends are made for leisurely lunches. This beauty is Italian but not as we know it – chef Dan Pepperell delivers a border-hopping menu that makes for a fetching Easter feast.

—

+ Devilled Easter eggs

+ Kingfish ham

+ Scampi "casino"

+ Anchovy fried rice

+ Braised rabbit with sauce pearà

+ Hot cross cannoli

+ Tiramisù

—

DEVILLED EASTER EGGS

"This is for everyone who knew how to throw a wild dinner party in the '60s and '70s, the era of English asparagus, cucumber sandwiches, prawn cocktails and devilled eggs," says Dan Pepperell. *"The smoked oil adds a new element to these eggs and a little extra umami always helps, here thanks to the bottarga."*

PREP TIME 20 MINS, COOK 10 MINS
SERVES 6-8

—

- 6 eggs, at room temperature
- 75 gm (¼ cup) Kewpie mayonnaise (see note)
- 1 tbsp sriracha sauce
- 1 small piece bottarga (about 10gm; see note)
- 1½ tbsp finely chopped chives

SMOKED OIL
- 2 tbsp olive oil
- 100 gm smoking woodchips, such as oak or applewood

1 For smoked oil, pour olive oil into a small metal container (a disposable pie dish works well), line a frying pan with foil, scatter woodchips over the base and heat over high heat until woodchips start to smoke (2-4 minutes). Push chips around the side of the pan to form a well in the centre, then place the dish of oil in the well, reduce heat to low, cover with a tight-fitting lid and smoke for 10 minutes. Remove oil and set aside to cool (discard chips when cooled).

2 Cook eggs in a large saucepan of boiling salted water, stirring gently at first so the yolk sets in the centre, until hard-boiled (10 minutes). Drain, cool under cold running water, then peel and halve lengthways. Remove yolks and push through a fine sieve into a bowl. Add mayonnaise, sriracha, and smoked olive oil, beat until creamy, season to taste, then transfer to a piping bag fitted with a 1cm-diameter star nozzle.

3 Pipe yolk mixture into the eggwhite halves, finely grate bottarga over the top and sprinkle with chives. Serve at room temperature. Devilled eggs can be made a day ahead and kept refrigerated.

NOTE Kewpie mayonnaise, a Japanese brand, is available from Asian grocers. Bottarga, the salted dried roe of either mullet or tuna, is available from select delicatessens.

WINE SUGGESTIONS A white sparkling or a bright, floral rosé.

EASTER AT 10 WILLIAM ST

EASTER AT 10 WILLIAM ST

KINGFISH HAM

"This dish came about while playing around with the idea of pairing prosciutto, which is basically cured and dried pork, with melon," says Pepperell. "We thought cured and dried kingfish could be an interestingly happy alternative." Start this recipe two days ahead to cure the kingfish.

PREP TIME 30 MINS (PLUS CURING)
SERVES 6-8

- 1 piece sashimi-grade kingfish top loin (about 600gm), bloodline trimmed, skinned (see note)
- Finely grated rind and juice of ½ lemon, ½ orange and ½ lime, plus extra lemon wedges to serve
- 150 gm each fine sea salt and caster sugar
- Extra-virgin olive oil, to serve
- 2-3 finger limes or blood limes, halved
- ½ rockmelon, seeded, cut into wedges, then bite-sized pieces

1 Place kingfish in a single layer in a non-reactive container (see cook's notes p279), then combine citrus rinds, juices, salt and sugar in a bowl, rub all over fish, cover and refrigerate for 2 hours, turning occasionally, until lightly cured. Rinse off salt and pat dry with paper towels, then wrap fish in muslin and hang up by a piece of string in the fridge for 48 hours. Cured kingfish will keep refrigerated, wrapped in plastic wrap, for a week.

2 Thinly slice kingfish across the grain and arrange on a plate, dress with a squeeze of lemon and extra-virgin olive oil, and serve with finger limes and a wedge of rockmelon.

NOTE You'll need to order kingfish top loin ahead from your fishmonger. Finger limes and blood limes are available from select greengrocers. If they're unavailable, substitute lime or lemon.

WINE SUGGESTIONS A white sparkling or a bright, floral rosé.

SCAMPI "CASINO"

"Clams casino is a super-traditional Italian-American classic, usually served on special occasions, holidays or in every single Italian restaurant in Little Italy in Manhattan," says Pepperell. "We thought, why not make it even more special and serve it with scampi instead? I love clams but scampi is one of my all-time favourite treats from the sea."

PREP TIME 25 MINS, COOK 1 HR 40 MINS
SERVES 6-8

—

1	head garlic
100	gm softened unsalted butter
1	small red capsicum
	Olive oil, for brushing
2	tbsp panko crumbs
80	gm mild pancetta, finely diced
3	golden shallots, finely chopped
	Olive oil, for frying
60	ml dry white wine
12	scampi, halved lengthways
1	tbsp chopped curly-leaf parsley
1	pinch gochugaru (see note) or other chilli flakes
	Lemon wedges, to serve

1 Preheat oven to 200C. Wrap garlic in foil and roast until very tender (30-40 minutes). When cool enough to handle, squeeze garlic from the skins into a bowl, add butter and mix well. This can be refrigerated in an airtight container for 2 days. Bring to room temperature before using.

2 Brush capsicum with oil and roast until softened and skin is blistered (30-35 minutes). Set aside to cool, then peel, core and dice.

3 Spread panko crumbs on an oven tray and toast in oven, stirring occasionally, until golden (7-10 minutes).

4 Sauté pancetta and shallot in a little oil in a frying pan over low-medium heat until shallot is translucent and softened (10-12 minutes). Deglaze pan with wine and simmer until evaporated (4-6 minutes), then stir in capsicum and remove from heat.

5 Arrange scampi on an oven tray flesh-side up. Top each with a little pancetta mixture, then garlic butter and roast until scampi are opaque and just cooked (6-10 minutes). Arrange on a plate, top with any remaining garlic butter and pancetta mixture, sprinkle with toasted panko crumbs, chopped parsley, gochugaru and a squeeze of lemon, season to taste and serve.

NOTE Gochugaru, Korean dried chilli, is available from Asian grocers.
WINE SUGGESTIONS A white sparkling or a bright, floral rosé.

EASTER AT 10 WILLIAM ST

DAN PEPPERELL

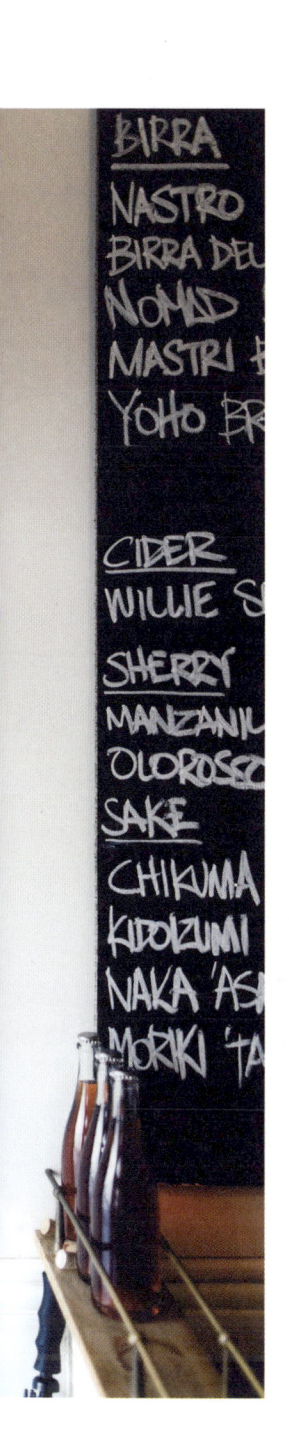

BIRRA
NASTRO
BIRRA DEL
NOMAD
MASTRI
YOHO BR

CIDER
WILLIE S

SHERRY
MANZANI
OLOROSO
SAKE
CHIKUMA
KIDOIZUMI
NAKA 'AS
MORIKI 'TA

EASTER AT 10 WILLIAM ST

ANCHOVY FRIED RICE

BRAISED RABBIT WITH
SAUCE PEARÀ

EASTER AT 10 WILLIAM ST

ANCHOVY FRIED RICE

"Fried rice is one of my favourite Chinese dishes," says Pepperell. "This is an Italian spin on it using colatura di alici and speck. Colatura di alici can be a bit pricey, but for a special occasion your guests will love the flavour. If you can't find it you can use salted anchovies or a high-quality fish sauce instead."

PREP TIME 10 MINS, COOK 10 MINS
SERVES 6-8

—

- 60 ml (¼ cup) peanut oil
- 3 eggs, half-beaten, leaving traces of eggwhite and yolk still visible
- 75 gm (½ cup) speck, finely diced
- ½ small onion, finely chopped
- 4 large garlic cloves, crushed
- 2 baby zucchini (or ½ small), thinly sliced
- 30 ml dry white wine
- 75 ml colatura di alici (see note)
- 3 tsp light soy sauce
- ¾ tsp caster sugar
- 650 gm (4½ cups) steamed medium-grain rice (about 3 cups uncooked)
- 4 spring onions, thinly sliced

1 Heat 20ml peanut oil in a non-stick wok over high heat, add egg and stir until scrambled and just cooked (2-3 minutes). Remove and set aside. Wipe out pan, add remaining oil and stir-fry speck, onion and garlic until aromatic and onion is translucent and just turning golden (2-4 minutes). Add zucchini and wine, and simmer until wine evaporates (30 seconds). Add colatura di alici, soy sauce and sugar, then add rice and spring onion, return egg to wok, toss until combined and rice is warmed through (2-3 minutes), then serve with extra colatura di alici for seasoning.
NOTE Colatura di alici, an Italian unfermented fish sauce made from anchovies, is available from select delicatessens.

BRAISED RABBIT WITH SAUCE PEARÀ

"We sometimes like to make this sauce on a winter's day for the family meal and serve it with chicken, in the absence of rabbit," says Pepperell.

PREP TIME 45 MINS, COOK 1½ HRS
SERVES 6-8

—

2½ tbsp olive oil
1 large rabbit (about 1.5kg), jointed into 8 pieces (see note)
10 garlic cloves, bruised
375 ml dry white wine
250 ml (1 cup) chicken stock
150 gm (1 cup) Ligurian olives in brine, pitted, and 200ml brine reserved
1 lemon, thickly sliced
1 cup (loosely packed) oregano
Chopped curly-leaf parsley, to serve

PEARÀ SAUCE
100 gm unsalted butter
100 gm beef bone marrow (see note)
50 gm dried porcini mushrooms soaked in 200ml cold water for 1 hour then coarsely chopped, water reserved separately
150 gm coarse sourdough breadcrumbs
100 ml chicken stock

1 Preheat oven to 200C. Heat oil in a large frying pan over medium-high heat, add rabbit in batches and lightly brown (2-3 minutes each side), then transfer to a flameproof roasting pan that fits rabbit pieces snugly in a single layer. Add garlic to frying pan and stir until pale golden (1 minute), then deglaze pan with wine and add to rabbit along with chicken stock and olive brine; the liquid should nearly cover the rabbit. Bring to a simmer on the stovetop, then add olives, lemon and oregano, season to taste with black pepper, then braise uncovered in oven until rabbit is cooked and sauce has thickened slightly (45 minutes to 1 hour). Season and keep warm.
2 For pearà sauce, heat butter and bone marrow in a frying pan over medium heat until mixture is bubbling (small pieces of marrow will remain visible; 4-6 minutes). Stir in porcini and cook until mushrooms smell nutty (2 minutes). Add breadcrumbs and stir over low heat until crumbs start to turn golden (10 minutes). Add reserved porcini water and chicken stock, simmer until stock slightly emulsifies with the fat and becomes the consistency of a wet bread sauce (1 minute). Season to taste.
3 Serve rabbit in bowls with lots of braising liquid and pearà sauce and scatter with parsley.
NOTE Order the rabbit in advance from your butcher and ask to have it jointed. Bone marrow is available from select butchers, but needs to be ordered ahead.
WINE SUGGESTIONS A skin-contact white (10 William St suggests a trebbiano-malvasia blend), or a gamay.

EASTER AT 10 WILLIAM ST

HOT CROSS CANNOLI

"Here we have the flavour profile of a hot cross bun in a cannolo," says Pepperell. "I like to think this is what Tony Soprano would eat at Easter time." Start this recipe a day ahead to rest the dough.

PREP TIME 25 MINS, COOK 15 MINS (PLUS RESTING)
SERVES 6-8

- 330 gm plain flour
- 1 tbsp Dutch-process cocoa powder
- 45 gm softened butter
- 45 gm pure icing sugar, plus extra for dusting
- 120 ml sweet Marsala (see note)
- 1 tsp white vinegar
- Grapeseed or vegetable oil, for deep-frying
- 1 egg, lightly beaten

RICOTTA FILLING
- 75 gm firm ricotta
- 25 gm caster sugar
- 50 gm mascarpone, beaten until smooth
- 2 tbsp currants
- 1 tbsp sultanas
- Finely grated rind of 1 lemon and 1 orange
- Pinch each of cinnamon and mixed spice

1 Rub together flour, cocoa and butter in a bowl with your fingertips until mixture resembles breadcrumbs. Add icing sugar, Marsala, vinegar and a pinch of salt, and mix to form a smooth dough. Wrap in plastic wrap and refrigerate overnight.

2 For ricotta filling, whisk ricotta and caster sugar in an electric mixer until smooth, then fold in mascarpone, dried fruit, rinds and spices. Transfer to a piping bag fitted with a 1cm-diameter plain nozzle and refrigerate until required.

3 Heat oil in a deep saucepan to 160C. Roll out dough on a lightly floured surface to 1mm thick (this can also be done with a pasta machine), cut out 11cm squares or rounds with a cutter, brush joining points with egg, wrap around a cannoli tube (see note) and press to seal (it's important that no egg touches the cannoli mould or it will stick). Remove from moulds and deep-fry cannoli tubes until golden and bubbled (30 seconds). Drain on paper towels and cool completely before piping in ricotta mixture. Dust with extra icing sugar and serve.

NOTE This recipe calls for quality Sicilian Marsala, rather than the more familiar Boronia all'uovo Marsala frequently used for cooking; it's available from select bottle shops including Dan Murphy's. Cannoli tubes are available from kitchenware shops; otherwise use dried cannelloni pasta tubes.

WINE SUGGESTION An elegant Marsala, such as Marco de Bartoli "Vigna la Miccia".

TIRAMISÙ

"An all-star Italian classic," says Pepperell. "This recipe doesn't use eggwhite, so has a slightly richer, more silky feel than most."

PREP TIME 15 MINS, COOK 10 MINS
SERVES 6-8

—

200 ml warm espresso
125 gm caster sugar
3 egg yolks
40 ml sweet Marsala (see note)
250 ml (1 cup) pouring cream
350 ml mascarpone
18 savoiardi biscuits (about a packet)
Dutch-process cocoa, sieved to serve

1 Stir coffee in a bowl with 50gm caster sugar to dissolve and set aside to cool.
2 Whisk egg yolks, Marsala and 25gm sugar in a heatproof bowl over a saucepan of gently simmering water until thick and mixture holds a thick ribbon (4-8 minutes). Whisk cream in an electric mixer with remaining sugar until soft-medium peaks form. Whisk mascarpone in a bowl to soften, add egg yolk mixture and gently combine, then add whipped cream and whisk to soft peaks.
3 Dip biscuits in cooled coffee, then arrange in a single layer in a 24cm baking dish. Cover with half the cream mixture, top with remaining coffee-soaked biscuits and spread remaining cream on top. Refrigerate until firm (2 hours). Serve chilled dusted with Dutch-process cocoa.
NOTE This recipe calls for quality Sicilian Marsala, rather than the more familiar Boronia Marsala all'Uovo frequently used for cooking; it's available from select bottle shops and Dan Murphy's.
WINE SUGGESTION An elegant Marsala, such as Marco de Bartoli "Vigna la Miccia".

EASTER AT 10 WILLIAM ST

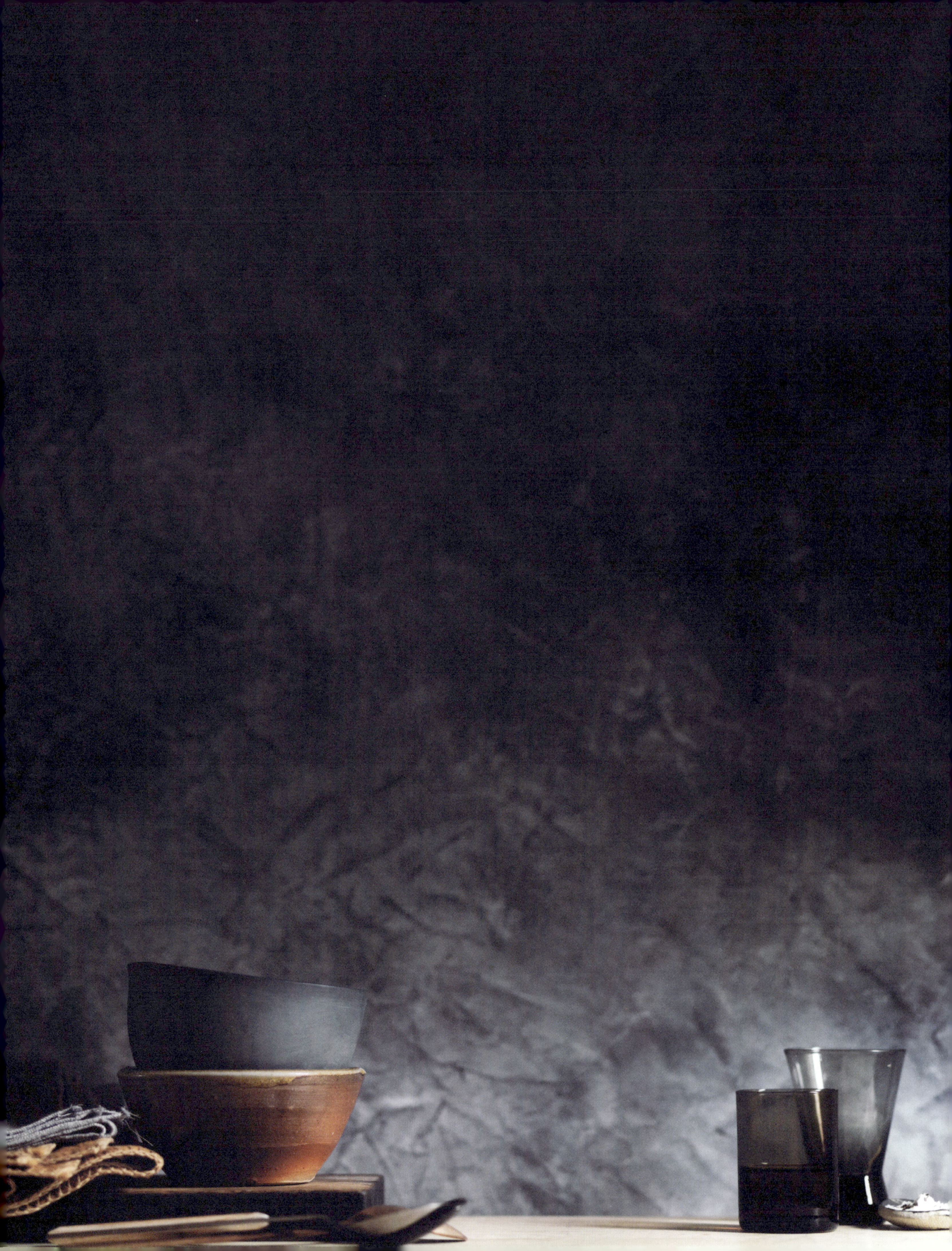

FIRESIDE SUPPER

The dark of winter calls for a rustic feast and a roaring fire. A centrepiece roast bookended by cheesy onion and bacon soup and a gingered-up self-saucing pud? Just say yes.

—

+ Onion and bacon soup with mustard and cheese crust

+ Radish, pear and seaweed salad with miso dressing

+ Beef rib roast with beetroot and horseradish

+ Goose-fat roast potatoes with dukkah

+ Carrots with garlic, ginger, spring onion and smoked chilli butter

+ Apple and candied ginger self-saucing pudding

+ Hot caramel and star anise milk

—

ONION AND BACON SOUP WITH MUSTARD AND CHEESE CRUST

This is a twist on the classic French onion soup. The key to its success is the wonderfully complex flavour of onion when it's given the time to unfurl fully, so don't try to stint on the cooking time – patience brings rewards.

PREP TIME 20 MINS, COOK 1¾ HRS
SERVES 6

—

- 100 gm butter, coarsely chopped
- 2 kg onions, thinly sliced
- 200 gm speck, cut into 1cm pieces
- 1 litre (4 cups) chicken stock
- 10 sage leaves, finely chopped
- 1 fresh bay leaf
- 6 thick slices ciabatta, toasted
- 300 gm coarsely grated cheddar
- 1 tbsp Dijon mustard

1 Melt butter in a large, wide saucepan over low heat, add onion and speck, cover and sauté gently, stirring occasionally, until onions are very soft (20-25 minutes). Remove lid and continue cooking, stirring occasionally, until starting to caramelise (50 minutes to 1 hour). Add ½ cup stock and simmer until almost evaporated (4-5 minutes), then repeat three times. Add remaining stock, sage and bay leaf, season to taste, bring to the boil, then reduce heat to low and simmer uncovered, scraping the base of the pan occasionally to remove any caramelised bits, until thick (8-10 minutes).

2 Preheat oven to 200C. Ladle soup into 1½-cup ovenproof bowls and transfer to an oven tray. Place a slice of toast on top of each. Mix cheese and mustard in a bowl and spoon a layer over the toast and soup. Bake until golden and bubbling (4-5 minutes) and serve.

DRINK SUGGESTION Medium-sweet scrumpy.

FIRESIDE SUPPER

FIRESIDE SUPPER

RADISH, PEAR AND SEAWEED SALAD WITH MISO DRESSING

Seaweed is the new black. The dried form can be found in the Asian section of supermarkets and keeps for a long time in the pantry. Have a few packets handy to add to salads like this, and experiment with mixing different kinds together. Given its ocean origin, this salad goes extremely well with all kinds of seafood.

PREP TIME 15 MINS
SERVES 6

---

50 gm dried wakame
700 gm radishes, trimmed, scrubbed and quartered
2 pears (such as Packham), cored, shaved on a mandolin

MISO DRESSING
1 tbsp light soy sauce
1 tbsp rice wine
1 tbsp cider vinegar
2 tbsp shiro miso

1 Place wakame in a large bowl, cover with warm water and soak for 5 minutes, then drain well. Combine radishes and pears in a large bowl, then add drained seaweed.
2 For miso dressing, combine soy sauce, rice wine and cider vinegar in a bowl with 2 tbsp water. Add miso and whisk to combine.
3 Arrange salad in a large serving bowl or on a platter, drizzle with miso dressing and serve.

GOOSE-FAT ROAST POTATOES
WITH DUKKAH

BEEF RIB ROAST WITH BEETROOT
AND HORSERADISH

FIRESIDE SUPPER

BEEF RIB ROAST WITH BEETROOT AND HORSERADISH

The earthiness of beetroot and horseradish is the perfect match to a perfectly roasted piece of beef, still pink and juicy.

PREP TIME 10 MINS, COOK 3 HRS 10 MINS
SERVES 6

—

900 gm (about 6) beetroot, scrubbed
60 ml (¼ cup) olive oil
2.4 kg beef rib roast, at room temperature
3 heads garlic, halved crossways
30 gm horseradish, freshly grated
240 gm (1 cup) sour cream

1 Preheat oven to 180C. Drizzle beetroot with half the olive oil and wrap individually in foil. Roast on an oven tray until tender when pierced with a skewer (1¼-1½ hours). Unwrap and allow to cool.
2 Increase oven temperature to 220C. Place beef in a roasting tray, drizzle with remaining oil and season to taste, rubbing all over to coat evenly. Roast for 30 minutes, then reduce oven to 150C and roast until cooked to your liking, adding garlic in last 15 minutes of cooking (about 1¼ hours for medium rare; with an internal temperature of 65C). Remove beef from the oven, cover loosely with foil and set aside for at least 10 minutes to rest.
3 Meanwhile, when beetroot are cool enough to handle, peel them and pulse in a food processor until finely chopped. Season to taste and stir in horseradish and sour cream.
4 Cut beef into cutlets and serve with garlic, beetroot and horseradish, and pan juices.
WINE SUGGESTION Big, bold Barossa cabernet.

GOOSE-FAT ROAST POTATOES WITH DUKKAH

The ultimate roast potato is crisp and golden on the outside, fluffy on the inside, and these tick all the boxes. The goose fat crisps up the outside, and using a floury potato ensures a fluffy centre.

PREP TIME 15 MINS, COOK 1 HR 10 MINS
SERVES 6

- 1.8 kg floury potatoes, such as kennebec or King Edward, peeled and halved or quartered if large
- 200 gm goose or duck fat
- 35 gm (¼ cup) plain flour
- Chopped flat-leaf parsley, to serve

DUKKAH
- 130 gm hazelnuts
- 80 gm sesame seeds
- 15 gm cumin seeds
- 15 gm coriander seeds
- 2 tbsp sea salt flakes
- 2 tbsp dried thyme

1 For dukkah, preheat oven to 180C. Spread hazelnuts on a baking tray and roast until toasted (8-10 minutes). Cool briefly, then tip into a tea towel and rub off skins. Meanwhile, spread sesame, cumin and coriander seeds on a separate tray and toast until fragrant (6-7 minutes). Coarsely crush hazelnuts, seeds, salt and thyme with a mortar and pestle and store in an airtight container until required. Dukkah will keep for 2 weeks.

2 Cover potatoes well with cold salted water in a saucepan, bring to the boil and cook uncovered until edges just begin to soften (10-15 minutes). Drain and set aside.

3 Preheat oven to 200C. Place fat in a roasting pan in the oven until hot. Dust potatoes in flour, roll in the fat to coat, then return the pan to the oven and roast, turning potatoes occasionally and basting them with goose fat, until golden brown and tender when pierced with a skewer (35-40 minutes). Scatter with dukkah to taste and parsley, and serve hot.

CARROTS WITH GARLIC, GINGER, SPRING ONION AND SMOKED CHILLI BUTTER

Keep the smoked chilli butter handy to spoon over almost any root vegetable as well as greens such as cabbage and kale, or even green beans and zucchini in summer.

PREP TIME 10 MINS, COOK 25 MINS
SERVES 6

—

- 1.5 kg baby carrots, trimmed and scrubbed
- 200 gm butter, coarsely chopped
- 8 garlic cloves, finely chopped
- 2 tbsp finely grated ginger
- 10 gm chipotle chillies, finely chopped (see note)
- 8 spring onions, thinly sliced

1 Bring a large saucepan of salted water to the boil, add carrots and cook until just tender (15-20 minutes). Drain and arrange on a platter.

2 Melt butter in a saucepan over medium heat, add garlic, ginger, chilli and spring onion and simmer briefly (1-2 minutes). Season to taste and spoon butter over carrots, then serve.

NOTE Chipotle chillies are available from Fireworks Foods (fireworksfoods.com.au) and select delicatessens.

FIRESIDE SUPPER

FIRESIDE SUPPER

APPLE AND CANDIED GINGER SELF-SAUCING PUDDING

When it's cold and windy outside, a pudding strikes all the right chords. This recipe also works well with pears.

PREP TIME 20 MINS, COOK 55 MINS
SERVES 6

—

800 gm (about 4) apples (such as Granny Smith or golden delicious), peeled, cored and each cut into 8 wedges
50 gm caster sugar
150 gm butter, melted, plus extra for greasing
190 gm (1¼ cups) self-raising flour
165 gm (¾ cup) brown sugar
125 ml (½ cup) milk
1 egg
45 gm crystallised ginger, thinly sliced
115 gm (⅓ cup) golden syrup
1 tbsp cornflour
Thickened cream or ice-cream and ground cinnamon, to serve

1 Cook apples, caster sugar and 50gm butter in a frying pan over medium-high heat, turning occasionally, until caramelised (7-8 minutes). Set aside to cool.
2 Preheat oven to 180C. Butter a 1.5-litre (6-cup) ovenproof dish or six 350ml shallow ovenproof bowls and spoon in apple mixture. Combine flour and 55gm brown sugar in a bowl, add milk, egg, ginger, 2 tbsp golden syrup and remaining butter, and stir until smooth, then spoon batter over apples, spreading to cover evenly.
3 Combine cornflour and remaining brown sugar in a bowl and sprinkle mixture over batter. Stir remaining golden syrup and 375ml boiling water in a jug and gently pour onto topping over the back of a spoon. Bake until golden brown and a skewer inserted comes out clean (40-45 minutes, or 20-25 minutes for individual puddings). Serve hot topped with cream or ice-cream and dusted with cinnamon.
WINE SUGGESTION Botrytised pinot gris.

HOT CARAMEL AND STAR ANISE MILK

Instead of a hot chocolate, why not try a hot caramel for a twist on the comforting classic? Make the caramel as far ahead as you wish, keep it in the fridge and have it with the warm milk as the mood takes you.

PREP TIME 5 MINS, COOK 15 MINS
SERVES 6

—

350 gm caster sugar
100 ml pouring cream
2 litres full-cream milk
1 vanilla bean, halved lengthways
4 star anise
Finely grated nutmeg, to serve

1 Cook sugar in a saucepan over medium-high heat until it begins to dissolve, swirl the pan and continue to boil until caramelised (5-10 minutes). Remove from heat and add cream (be careful, hot caramel will spit). Return saucepan to heat and stir until caramel dissolves.
2 Warm milk in a saucepan with vanilla bean and star anise over a low heat until milk comes almost to the boil, then strain.
3 Spoon a little caramel into serving cups, top with milk, dust with nutmeg and serve.
DRINK SUGGESTION Add a splash of Armagnac.

FIRESIDE SUPPER

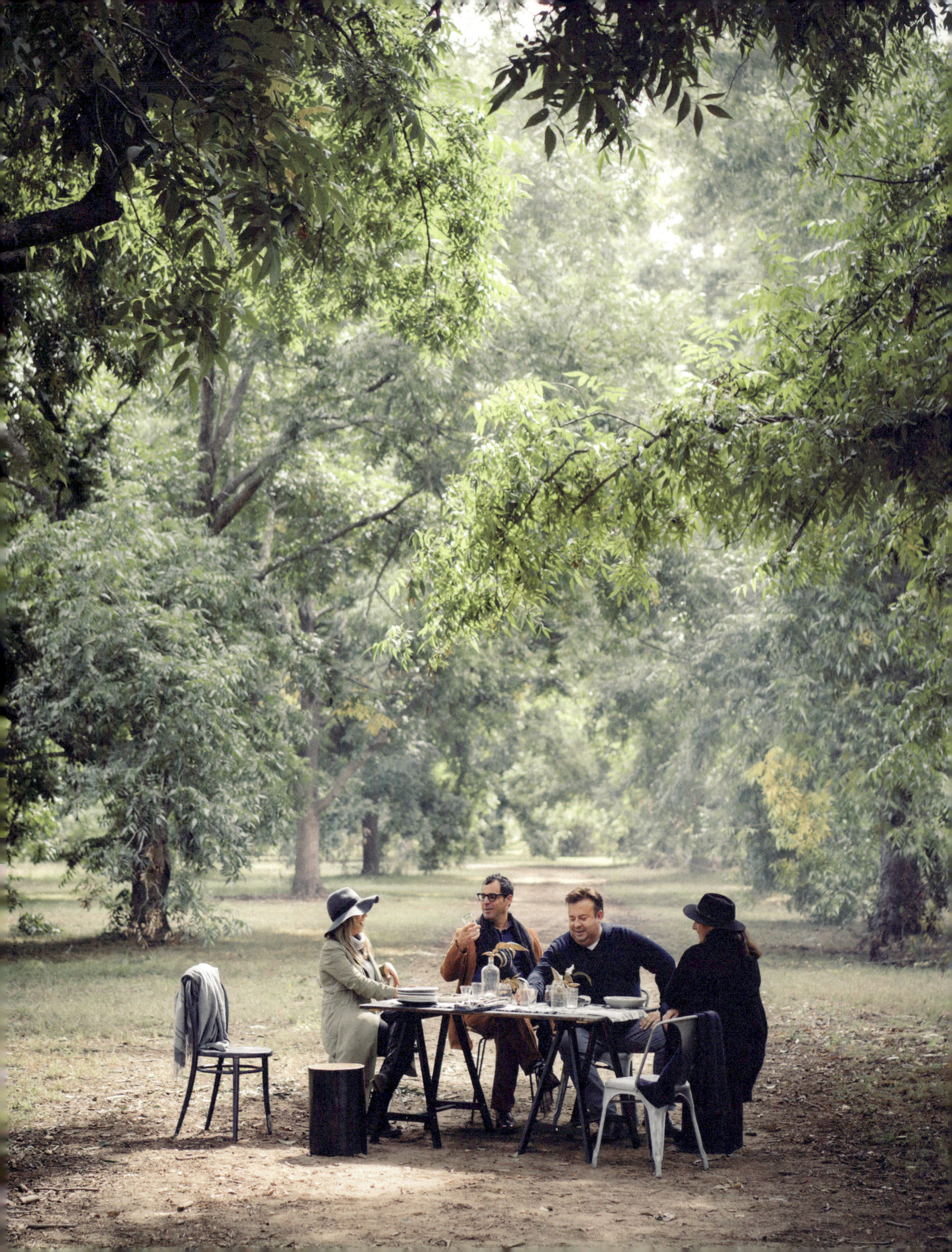

SUNDAY LUNCH WITH PETER GILMORE

One of Australia's finest chefs, Quay's Peter Gilmore puts big, bold flavours to the fore in this indulgent wintry menu. Treat yourself to silky smoked chestnut soup and grilled wagyu rump cap before finishing on a ridiculously decadent trifle. Pull up a chair.

—

+ Smoky chestnut soup

+ Grilled marron on a stick with citrus butter, flowers and herbs

+ Salt-baked pumpkin with Pyengana cream and toasted grains

+ Grilled wagyu rump cap

+ Roasted carrots with feta, almonds and sherry caramel

+ Grilled shiitake mushrooms with umami butter

+ Winter greens salad

+ Quince, pecan and crème caramel trifle with Gretchen's honey cream

—

SMOKY CHESTNUT SOUP

"I like to serve this soup in cups while guests are gathered before lunch," says Peter Gilmore. Skip the smoking for a clearer chestnut flavour.

PREP TIME 30 MINS, COOK 1 HR 10 MINS (PLUS COOLING)
SERVES 8

—

- 350 gm chestnuts (about 16; see note)
- 50 gm (about ⅔ cup) smoking woodchips, such as hickory or maple (see note)
- 100 gm unsalted butter, coarsely chopped
- 2 celery stalks from the pale inner heart, finely chopped
- 3 golden shallots, finely chopped
- 2 garlic cloves, finely chopped
- 2 litres (8 cups) chicken stock
- 1 turnip, peeled and coarsely chopped
- 150 ml pouring cream

1 Preheat oven to 180C. Score a cross in the top of each chestnut with a small sharp knife just to the flesh (so they don't explode during cooking). Roast chestnuts on a wire rack in the oven until the cuts open up (15-20 minutes). Transfer to a heatproof bowl, cover with foil and leave to steam for 10-15 minutes, then peel away the chestnuts' outer and inner layers to expose the soft nut. Turn off the oven to cool.

2 Set chestnuts on a wire rack on the top shelf of the cold oven or a barbecue with a lid. Place woodchips in a cast-iron frying pan and light with a large blowtorch, allow to burn for a couple of minutes, then blow out the flames. Place the smoking woodchips in the oven on a shelf below the chestnuts (or in barbecue, with the vents closed), close the door and leave until chestnuts are smoky flavoured, relighting and extinguishing woodchips if they stop smoking (20-25 minutes; check after 10 minutes).

3 Meanwhile, melt half the butter in a large saucepan over medium heat, add celery, shallot and garlic, and sauté until onion is translucent (3-4 minutes). Add stock, turnip and smoked chestnuts, increase heat and boil until stock reduces by half and vegetables are soft (30-40 minutes). Add remaining butter and blend in a food processor or with a hand-held blender until smooth. Season to taste and strain through a fine sieve for extra smoothness. This soup can be made 2 days ahead.

4 To serve, bring the soup to a simmer over medium-high heat. Whisk cream to soft peaks, reserve a quarter, and whisk remaining through the soup. Serve in cups topped with a dollop of cream and freshly ground black pepper to taste.

NOTE Choose lighter-coloured chestnuts for easier peeling. Smoking woodchips are available from specialist barbecue shops and online from bbqaroma.com.

WINE SUGGESTIONS An Australian blanc de blancs, or brut Champagne.

SUNDAY LUNCH WITH PETER GILMORE

SUNDAY LUNCH WITH PETER GILMORE

GRILLED MARRON ON A STICK WITH CITRUS BUTTER, FLOWERS AND HERBS

"King prawns also work nicely for this recipe," says Gilmore. "It's a fun way to get your guests involved by inviting them to finish their skewer with fresh herbs and flowers." Soak eight bamboo skewers in water for at least 30 minutes before cooking.

**PREP TIME 20 MINS, COOK 5 MINS
(PLUS PREPARING COALS, FREEZING)
SERVES 8**

—

- 8 (150gm each) live marron (see note), or 8 large uncooked king prawns
- 2 tbsp mixed edible flower petals
- 1 tbsp small fennel fronds (optional)
- 1 tbsp (loosely packed) chervil leaves
- 1 tbsp finely chopped chives

CITRUS BUTTER
- 80 gm unsalted cultured butter, softened
- Finely grated rind of ½ lemon and ½ lime

1 If you're cooking over a fire, light the wood or coals and let the fire burn down to hot embers (1–1½ hours); otherwise heat a barbecue when you're making the citrus butter.

2 Place marron in the freezer to render them insensible (50 minutes to 1 hour; see cook's notes p279), then cook them in a large saucepan of rapidly boiling salted water for 1 minute. Refresh in iced water, then remove the tails and cut the shells down the centre over the belly with scissors and remove tail meat. Skewer on soaked bamboo skewers (for prawns, peel, remove heads and devein, then thread onto skewers). Cover and refrigerate until required.

3 For citrus butter, mix butter and rinds together in a bowl and season to taste. Transfer to a small dish and leave at room temperature.

4 Mix flowers, fennel fronds and herbs and place in a dish. Season marron and grill, turning occasionally, until almost cooked through but still a fraction translucent in the centre (1 minute each side). Serve to guests to roll in the butter and sprinkle with the flowers and herbs.

NOTE Live marron need to be ordered ahead from a fishmonger, or from your local fish market.

WINE SUGGESTIONS An aromatic viognier blend such as Thick as Thieves "Fancy Pants", or a Victorian roussanne.

SALT-BAKED PUMPKIN WITH PYENGANA CREAM AND TOASTED GRAINS

"This is an impressive entrée to bring to the table," says Gilmore. "Crack open the crust at the table so your guests get the scent of pumpkin, then take it to the kitchen to finish the presentation." Gilmore bakes the pumpkin in a firepit of hot coals, but has given an oven method, too. If you're cooking it in a firepit, prepare it a few hours ahead so you have a deep layer of hot coals.

PREP TIME 40 MINS, COOK 2 HRS
(PLUS PREPARING FIREPIT, RESTING)
SERVES 8-10

—

- 1 small Kent or medium potimarron pumpkin (1.5kg-2.25kg; see note)
- Rock salt, for baking
- 2 tbsp pepitas
- 2 tbsp sunflower seeds
- 50 gm unsalted butter, coarsely chopped
- 30 gm (1¼ cups) puffed quinoa (see note)
- 30 gm (½ cup) puffed barley (see note)
- 30 gm (½ cup) puffed wild rice (see note)

SALT-CRUST DOUGH
- 600 gm (4 cups) plain flour
- 300 gm sea salt
- 120 gm eggwhite (about 4)

PYENGANA CHEDDAR CREAM
- 20 gm finely chopped golden shallots (1-2 shallots)
- 1 garlic clove, finely chopped
- 20 gm unsalted butter
- 400 ml pouring cream
- 150 gm Pyengana cheddar, or another hard cheese, finely grated

1 For salt-crust dough, mix flour, salt, eggwhite and 250ml cold water in an electric mixer fitted with a dough hook until the mixture comes together, then transfer to a floured work surface and knead until smooth (2-3 minutes). Wrap in plastic wrap and rest for 1 hour.

2 If you're using the oven, preheat oven to 190C. Roll out salt-crust dough to 5mm thick, place pumpkin in the centre and wrap in dough to encase it completely, pinching edges to seal. Pierce two small holes in the top of the pumpkin with a skewer, through pastry and into the flesh, to allow steam to escape. Place pumpkin on a bed of rock salt in a baking dish and bake (or bury in the hot coals of the firepit) until pumpkin is cooked and the internal temperature on an inserted probe thermometer reaches 85C (1¼ hours for a 1.5kg pumpkin and up to 1¾ hours for 2.25kg pumpkin). Set aside to rest for 20 minutes, then place on a tray or plate and crack open the pastry.

3 Meanwhile, for Pyengana cream, sauté shallot and garlic in butter in a saucepan over low heat until soft and translucent (8-10 minutes). Add cream, increase heat, bring to the boil and cook until reduced by a third (3-4 minutes). Reduce heat to very low, scatter in cheddar and whisk until melted. Keep warm, or reheat gently to serve.

4 Reduce oven to 180C. Roast pepitas and sunflower seeds on an oven tray lined with baking paper or on a silicone oven tray until light golden (6-8 minutes). Set aside to cool. Melt butter in a non-stick frying pan over medium-high heat until foaming. Add puffed quinoa, barley and wild rice, toss to coat, then add roasted pepitas and sunflower seeds, and toss to combine and warm through (30-40 seconds). Season to taste and mix for a minute off the heat. Keep warm or gently reheat to serve.

5 Slice pumpkin into wedges, remove seeds and fibrous centre and peel the skin away with a knife. The pumpkin should be meltingly soft and tender. Place a wedge on each serving plate, spoon cheese sauce on top, sprinkle generously with grains and seeds and serve.

NOTE Potimarron, a French heirloom pumpkin, is available from Johnstone's Kitchen Gardens (johnstonefarmer.com) and farmers' markets. Puffed quinoa and barley are available from health-food shops or royalnutcompany.com.au. For puffed wild rice, deep-fry 25gm uncooked wild rice for 10-20 seconds at 190C, then remove with a fine skimmer or drain in a sieve and cool on paper towels; otherwise use regular puffed rice.

WINE SUGGESTIONS A restrained chardonnay such as Canobolas-Smith "Shine", or a rosé like KT Rosé.

SUNDAY LUNCH WITH PETER GILMORE

SUNDAY LUNCH WITH PETER GILMORE

GRILLED WAGYU RUMP CAP

"The wagyu can be replaced with a good cut of Angus beef," says Gilmore. "The important thing is to use a large piece of beef so you can carve it at the table."

PREP TIME 5 MINS, COOK 1 HR (PLUS PREPARING COALS)
SERVES 8

—

- 1 wagyu rump cap or well-marbled Black Angus rump cap (1.6kg; see note), removed from fridge 40 minutes before cooking
- Grapeseed or olive oil, for brushing
- 150 ml veal glaze (see note), warmed

1 Heat a charcoal barbecue with a lid until very hot coals form (15-30 minutes). If using a barbecue without a lid, also preheat the oven to 180C. Brush beef with oil and season to taste, then grill, turning regularly, until browned (1-2 minutes each side). Transfer beef to a wire rack in a roasting pan and place away from the coals to cook indirectly, close the lid and bring the barbecue to 180C, or roast in oven, turning once halfway through, until cooked to your liking (40 minutes to 1 hour for medium-rare, with an internal temperature of 55C). Loosely cover beef with foil and rest for 15-20 minutes. Carve beef, brush with warmed veal glaze and serve.

NOTE You'll need to order wagyu or Black Angus rump cap ahead from a butcher. If you can't source this cut, use another large roasting beef joint such as rib-eye. Veal glaze is available from specialty butcher shops.

WINE SUGGESTIONS A shiraz such as La Violetta "La Ciornia", or a grenache such as Ochota Barrels "The Fugazi Vineyard".

230 GOURMET TRAVELLER | MENUS

SUNDAY LUNCH WITH PETER GILMORE

SUNDAY LUNCH WITH PETER GILMORE

ROASTED CARROTS WITH FETA, ALMONDS AND SHERRY CARAMEL

"The key to the success of this salad, my all-time favourite, is the sherry caramel – it's luscious, sweet and tart all at once," says Gilmore. "The interplay of texture with crunchy almonds, sweet roasted carrots and creamy feta is simply delicious." This recipe makes more sherry caramel than you need, but it keeps well (for at least a month covered and refrigerated); use it to dress other salads and roasted vegetables.

PREP TIME 40 MINS, COOK 45 MINS
SERVES 8

- 12 long carrots (1.6kg), peeled
- 200 ml extra-virgin olive oil
- 200 gm natural almonds, split in half with a small knife along the seam
- 300 gm Meredith goat's feta, or sheep's milk feta
- 25 gm (½ cup) puffed amaranth (see note)
- ¼ cup edible flowers (see note)

SHERRY CARAMEL
- 150 gm caster sugar
- 375 ml (1½ cups) oloroso sherry
- 180 ml sherry vinegar

1 For sherry caramel, stir sugar and 300ml sherry in a deep saucepan over medium heat until sugar dissolves (1-2 minutes). Increase heat to high and boil without stirring until a medium-dark caramel forms or mixture reaches 160C on a sugar thermometer (12-15 minutes). Add remaining sherry (be careful, hot caramel will spit), then stir while returning to the boil. Remove from heat, add sherry vinegar and stir thoroughly with a whisk. Cool completely before using; it should have the consistency of golden syrup once cooled. Makes 1½ cups.

2 Preheat oven to 180C. Boil carrots briefly until lightly cooked (2 minutes). Drain, toss with 50ml extra-virgin olive oil, season and roast on an oven tray lined with baking paper or on a silicone tray until soft (25-30 minutes). Cool completely (20-30 minutes).

3 Roast almonds on an oven tray lined with baking paper or on a silicone tray until golden brown (3-4 minutes). Cool completely.

4 Crumble feta over a platter. Cut carrots into 3cm pieces and toss in a bowl with 50ml extra-virgin olive oil, season to taste, and scatter carrots over the feta. Dress almonds in 50ml extra-virgin olive oil, season to taste and scatter on top of carrots. Scatter with puffed amaranth, drizzle with 2 tbsp sherry caramel, or to taste, then drizzle with remaining oil, garnish with flowers and serve.

NOTE Puffed amaranth is available from health-food shops. Edible flowers are available from select delicatessens, greengrocers and farmers' markets.

GRILLED SHIITAKE MUSHROOMS WITH UMAMI BUTTER

"I love the texture and flavour of shiitake mushrooms," says Gilmore. "If you can't find good shiitakes, then use large Swiss brown or flat mushrooms."

PREP TIME 15 MINS, COOK 5 MINS (PLUS PREPARING COALS)
SERVES 8

—

- 8 large or 16 small shiitake mushrooms
- Grapeseed or olive oil, for brushing

UMAMI BUTTER
- 40 gm unsalted butter, softened
- 3 gm (6cm-square piece) dried konbu, finely ground in a spice grinder (see note)
- ¼ dried shiitake mushroom, finely ground in a spice grinder
- 1 tsp roasted sesame seeds
- ¼ tsp fish sauce
- ¼ tsp finely grated lemon rind
- ¼ tsp white (shiro) miso paste

1 Heat a barbecue (20-30 minutes), or prepare a wood or coal fire, burning coals down to hot embers (1-1½ hours).

2 For umami butter, place butter in a bowl with ¾ tsp ground konbu, ¼ tsp ground shiitake (you may have a little remaining) and remaining ingredients, and mix well.

3 Trim and discard tough stems from mushrooms, brush with oil, season with salt to taste and grill over high heat, turning occasionally, until golden brown and tender (4-6 minutes).

4 To serve, arrange hot mushrooms on a platter gill-side up and top each with a teaspoonful of umami butter.

NOTE Konbu, dried kelp, is available from Japanese and Asian supermarkets.

SUNDAY LUNCH WITH PETER GILMORE

SUNDAY LUNCH WITH PETER GILMORE

WINTER GREEN SALAD

"This salad is a good foil for the rich beef," says Gilmore. "Use any mixture of winter greens – the more you can find, the more interesting the salad."

PREP TIME 15 MINS
SERVES 8

---

6 cups (loosely packed) mixed green winter leaves, such as young cavolo nero, nasturtium, winter purslane, chicory heart, red-veined dandelion, sorrel, salty ice plant, baby kale, young spinach or cabbage heart

RED WINE VINAIGRETTE

25 ml red wine vinegar
1 golden shallot, finely chopped
½ garlic clove, finely chopped
75 ml olive oil

1 For red wine vinaigrette, combine vinegar, shallot, garlic and a pinch of salt in a bowl, and set aside to macerate for 30 minutes, then whisk in olive oil and season with a few grinds of black pepper.

2 To serve, dress the winter leaves in a large bowl and toss lightly to coat.

QUINCE, PECAN AND CRÈME CARAMEL TRIFLE WITH GRETCHEN'S HONEY CREAM

"A centrepiece dessert that you serve to your guests at the table is a wonderful gesture of hospitality and generosity," says Gilmore. "Trifle is a classic, and served in a beautiful glass bowl it gives the lunch a sense of occasion." This recipe calls for eight individual metal pudding moulds for making the crème caramels, the custard element in this trifle. Start a day ahead to prepare the crèmes and the quince and jelly, and to soak the currants. The honey cream is named for the late Gretchen Wheen, a well-known beekeeper who used to own the property where this lunch was set.

**PREP TIME 1½ HRS, COOK 4 HRS 40 MINS
(PLUS RESTING, COOLING, CHILLING)
SERVES 8-10**

- 50 gm couverture white chocolate (such as Callebaut or Valrhona), cut into 4 pieces
- 150 gm (1¼ cups) pecans
- 50 gm currants, soaked in 150ml Pedro Ximénez sherry or Port overnight

CRÈME CARAMEL
- Grapeseed oil, for brushing
- 380 gm (⅔ cup) caster sugar
- 180 gm egg yolks (about 10 yolks)
- 2 eggs
- 1 litre (4 cups) milk

POACHED QUINCE AND JELLY
- 150 gm caster sugar
- 1 vanilla bean, split, seeds scraped
- 2 large quince
- 2 titanium-strength gelatine leaves, softened in cold water for 3 minutes

SPONGE CAKE
- 150 gm (⅔ cup) caster sugar
- 6 eggs
- 150 gm (1 cup) plain flour, sieved

GRETCHEN'S HONEY CREAM
- 375 ml (1½ cups) pouring cream
- 1½ tbsp honey, such as Australian bush honey or thyme-flower honey

1 For crème caramel, preheat oven to 160C and lightly oil eight 220ml metal pudding moulds. Stir 200gm sugar with 100ml water in a saucepan over medium-high heat until sugar dissolves, then boil without stirring until dark golden (6-8 minutes). Pour enough caramel into each mould to just cover the base and stand until set (10-15 minutes). Whisk yolks, eggs, and remaining sugar in a bowl until just pale (1-2 minutes). Meanwhile, bring milk close to boiling in a saucepan over medium-high heat, then, while whisking, pour milk onto eggs and sugar and whisk to combine. Strain mixture through a fine sieve into a jug. Place moulds in a deep roasting pan lined with a tea towel (to prevent moulds sliding), divide custard evenly among moulds, then fill pan with hot water to come halfway up the sides of moulds. Cover with foil and bake until caramels are set and barely wobble in the centre when gently shaken (40 minutes to 1 hour). Remove from oven, cool in the water bath for 10 minutes, then refrigerate overnight to chill. Dip moulds in hot water, then turn out and cut each into quarters.

2 For poached quince and jelly, whisk sugar, vanilla bean and seeds, and 500ml water in a flameproof casserole and bring to a simmer, stirring until sugar dissolves. Meanwhile, peel and halve quince, add to casserole, cover and poach in oven until tender and pink (2-3 hours). Remove quince from syrup, cover and refrigerate until required. Bring 200ml syrup (discard remainder) and 200ml water to the boil in a saucepan, squeeze excess water from gelatine and, off the heat, stir into syrup until dissolved. Strain syrup into a 500ml container and refrigerate until set (2-3 hours).

3 Meanwhile, for sponge cake, preheat oven to 160C and line a 10cm-deep, 23cm-square cake tin with baking paper. Whisk sugar and eggs in an electric mixer until thick and pale with a fine, firm foam (8-9 minutes). Sift in flour and fold to combine, then pour into prepared tin, spreading evenly. Bake until a skewer inserted withdraws with dry crumbs (20-25 minutes). Turn sponge out onto a rack to cool (20-30 minutes). Cake is best made on the day, but can be made a day ahead and wrapped in plastic wrap to keep fresh.>

SUNDAY LUNCH WITH PETER GILMORE

(continued)

4 Increase oven to 170C. Bake white chocolate pieces on an oven tray lined with baking or a silicone oven tray until chocolate is light caramel in colour (6-8 minutes). Cool completely, place in an airtight container, and refrigerate until required.

5 Roast pecans on an oven tray until crisp (7-8 minutes). Set aside to cool, then break with your hands, leaving some whole to decorate the top.

6 For honey cream, whisk cream and honey in a bowl until soft peaks form.

7 Core and thickly slice the quince, and cut or tear the sponge into 5cm pieces. To assemble, layer a 5-litre trifle bowl with half each of the pieces of sponge, currants and soaking liquid, quince jelly, crème caramel, sliced quince, crumbled pecans and honey cream. Repeat with remaining ingredients, then cover trifle and refrigerate to chill and set (2-3 hours).

8 To serve, coarsely grate caramelised white chocolate over the top and garnish with pecans.

WINE SUGGESTION A botrytised sémillon.

PETER GILMORE

SUNDAY LUNCH WITH PETER GILMORE

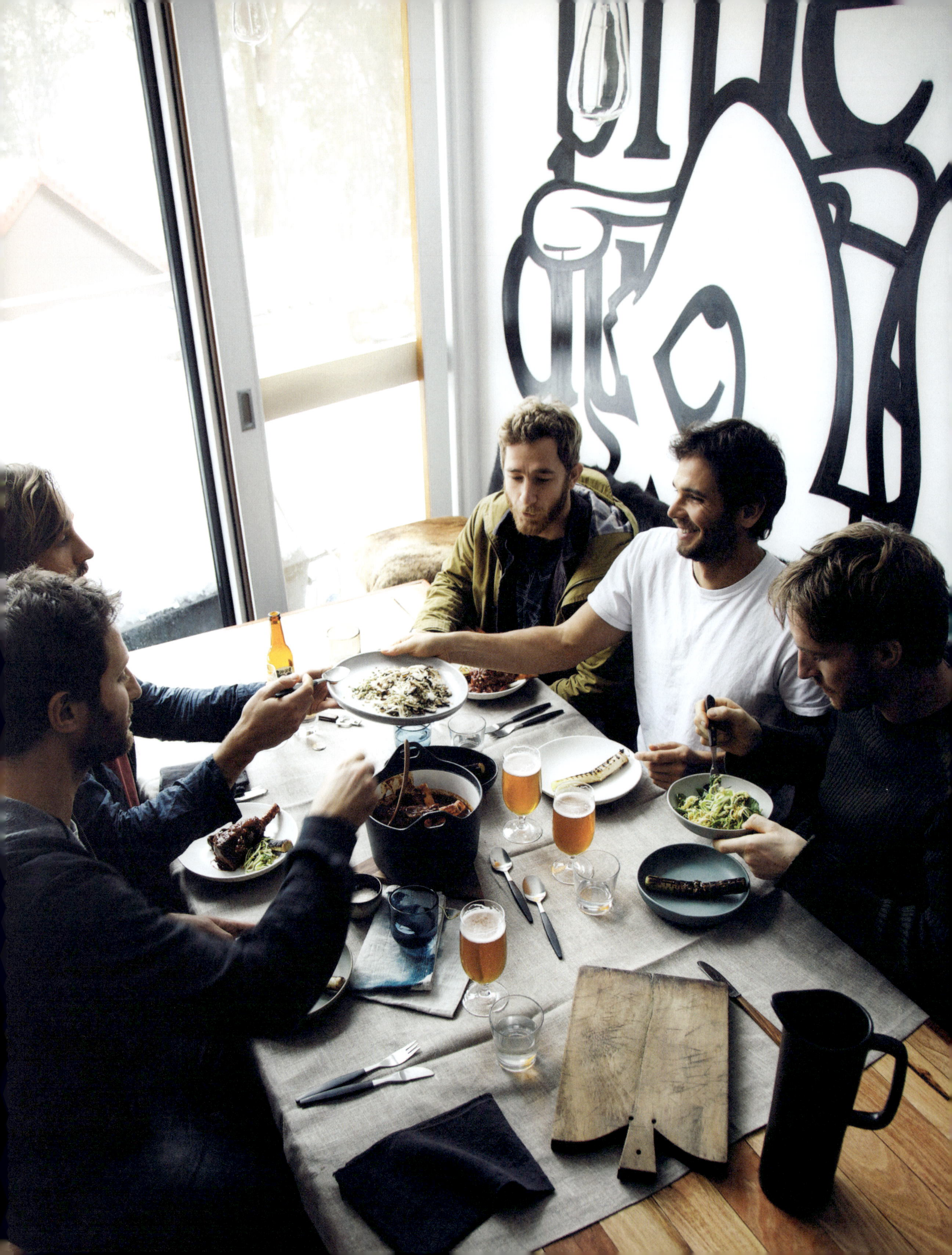

APRÈS-SKI WITH THE THREE BLUE DUCKS

Heading to the slopes? You'll want to hunker down with rib-sticking dishes designed to fill the hole after a day on the mountain. Darren Robertson, Mark LaBrooy and the Three Blue Ducks crew deliver a menu full of gutsy flavours pitch-perfect for the snowfields (or your next winter dinner party).

—

+ Parsnip and artichoke soup

+ Smoked trout, Dutch carrots and butter sauce

+ Mushrooms and grains

+ Braised lamb shanks, burnt leeks and zucchini salad

+ Beef cheeks with radish, mustard seed and pickled celery salad

+ Rice pudding

—

PARSNIP AND ARTICHOKE SOUP

PREP TIME 20 MINS, COOK 1 HR 10 MINS
SERVES 6

—

500 gm parsnips (about 2), trimmed, scrubbed
500 gm Jerusalem artichokes (about 7), scrubbed
2½ tbsp olive oil, plus extra to serve
1 thyme sprig
1 tsp butter
3 golden shallots, thinly sliced
1 garlic clove, thinly sliced
1.25 litres (5 cups) chicken stock
2 tbsp pouring cream, or to taste
20 gm (¼ cup) finely grated Parmigiano-Reggiano, plus extra to serve
1 tsp lemon juice
Finely grated rind of ¼ lemon

1 Preheat oven to 180C. Chop parsnip and artichoke into rough 5cm pieces, spread on an oven tray lined with baking paper, drizzle with half the oil, add thyme, season to taste and roast until golden and tender (35-45 minutes).
2 Heat butter and remaining oil in a saucepan over low-medium heat, add shallot and garlic, and sauté until tender (8 minutes), then add stock, bring to a simmer, add roast vegetables and simmer until tender (10-15 minutes). Remove from heat, remove thyme sprig, add cream, parmesan, lemon juice and rind, and process in a blender or with a hand-held blender until smooth, adding a little water if the soup is too thick. Season to taste, top with extra oil and parmesan to taste and serve hot.
WINE SUGGESTION A taut, crisp pinot grigio.

APRÈS-SKI WITH THE THREE BLUE DUCKS

APRÈS-SKI WITH THE THREE BLUE DUCKS

SMOKED TROUT, DUTCH CARROTS AND BUTTER SAUCE

"This recipe is great as it lets us use the baby carrots, shallots and dill growing in our garden," says Shannon Debreceny. "The flavour of the smoked trout and burnt shallots is a wonderful combination."

PREP TIME 30 MINS, COOK 15 MINS (PLUS RESTING)
SERVES 6

- 2 tbsp olive oil
- 12 Dutch carrots, scrubbed
- 6 spring onions, trimmed
- 6 smoked rainbow trout fillets (180gm each), skin on, pin-boned
- ½ cup (loosely packed) dill sprigs

BUTTER SAUCE
- 50 ml rice wine vinegar
- 2 egg yolks
- 1 tbsp honey
- 1 tsp caster sugar
- 150 gm butter, melted
- Juice and finely grated rind of ½ lemon

1 Heat 3 tsp oil in a large frying pan over high heat, add carrots and fry, turning occasionally, until just tender (2-3 minutes). Set aside.

2 Brush spring onions with 1 tsp oil, season to taste, place on a wire rack over a gas flame and cook, turning occasionally, until lightly charred (2-3 minutes; see note). Transfer to a bowl, cover with plastic wrap and steam until tender (2-3 minutes), then coarsely chop and set aside.

3 Heat remaining oil in a large non-stick frying pan over medium-high heat, add trout in batches skin-side down and cook until skin is golden (40 seconds to 1 minute), then turn and cook until warmed through (10 seconds). Transfer to a tray and keep warm.

4 For butter sauce, whisk vinegar, yolks, honey and sugar in a heatproof bowl over a saucepan of simmering water until starting to thicken (2 minutes; 70C on a thermometer). Season to taste, then, whisking continuously, gradually add melted butter in a thin steady stream. Add lemon juice and rind, season to taste and keep warm.

5 Serve trout, spring onion and carrots topped with butter sauce and dill.

NOTE If you don't have a gas burner, preheat grill to high and grill spring onions, turning occasionally, until lightly charred (2-3 minutes).

WINE SUGGESTION A mineral-rich chardonnay.

MUSHROOMS AND GRAINS

BRAISED LAMB SHANKS, BURNT LEEKS AND ZUCCHINI SALAD

APRÈS-SKI WITH THE THREE BLUE DUCKS

MUSHROOMS AND GRAINS

"This dish has been a favourite in Bronte," says Darren Robertson. "Grant, our gardener, grows a lot of our mushrooms, so we get to try them straight from the garden. This dish also works really well with other mushroom varieties; if you can't get your hands on shiitakes, king brown, nameko and wood-ear mushrooms also make interesting variations."

PREP TIME 40 MINS, COOK 45 MINS (PLUS COOLING)
SERVES 6

—

- 100 gm (½ cup) whole spelt (see note)
- 100 gm (½ cup) roasted buckwheat (see note)
- Juice and finely grated rind of 1 lemon
- 3 flat-leaf parsley sprigs, coarsely chopped
- 2 tbsp olive oil
- 1 golden shallot, finely chopped
- 1 garlic clove, finely chopped
- 50 gm shiitake mushrooms, thinly sliced
- 50 gm enoki mushrooms, trimmed

AJO BLANCO
- 50 gm blanched almonds
- 100 gm crustless sourdough bread
- 125 ml (½ cup) milk
- 1 tbsp olive oil
- 1 garlic clove, finely chopped
- Juice and finely grated rind of ¼ lemon

1 For ajo blanco, preheat oven to 180C. Roast almonds on an oven tray until golden (6-8 minutes), then set aside to cool. Soak bread in milk in a bowl until softened (2-3 minutes). Transfer to a blender, add roast almonds, oil, garlic, lemon juice and rind, and season to taste, then blend to a smooth thick paste, adding extra milk if necessary. Set aside. Makes about 250ml.

2 Cook spelt in a saucepan of lightly salted boiling water until just tender (18-20 minutes), drain, reserving cooking water, and transfer to a bowl. Return cooking water to pan, bring to the boil, add buckwheat and cook until just tender (10 minutes). Drain (discard cooking water), combine with spelt, season to taste, add lemon juice and rind, parsley and half the oil, and keep warm.

3 Heat remaining oil in a frying pan over low-medium heat, add shallot and garlic, and sauté until softened (4-5 minutes). Increase heat to high, add shiitakes and sauté until just starting to soften (40 seconds), then add enoki and stir until just warmed through (10 seconds). Season to taste and remove from heat. Transfer grains to a platter, top with mushrooms and dollops of ajo blanco and serve warm or at room temperature.

NOTE Whole spelt and roasted buckwheat are available from select health-food shops and delicatessens.

WINE SUGGESTION Pinot noir.

BRAISED LAMB SHANKS, BURNT LEEKS AND ZUCCHINI SALAD

"On a winter's night, who doesn't love lamb shanks?" asks Debreceny. "They're slow-braised till the sticky meat falls from the bone and finished off with the textural umami flavour of parmesan crumbs. It's the perfect dish to enjoy at home."

PREP TIME 40 MINS, COOK 4 HRS 10 MINS (PLUS COOLING)
SERVES 6

—

- 50 gm (⅔ cup) finely grated Parmigiano-Reggiano
- 50 gm blanched almonds
- 6 small leeks, tops trimmed
- 4 zucchini, cut into julienne on a mandolin
- ½ cup (loosely packed) each basil and mint leaves, torn
- 2 tbsp lemon juice, or to taste
- 3 tsp olive oil
- 1 tsp caster sugar

BRAISED LAMB SHANKS
- 1 tbsp grapeseed oil
- 6 large French-trimmed lamb shanks (350gm each)
- 1.2 kg canned whole tomatoes
- 1 litre red wine
- 750 ml (3 cups) chicken stock
- 140 gm tomato paste
- 3 each rosemary and thyme sprigs
- 2 garlic cloves, thinly sliced
- ½ long red chilli, thinly sliced

1 For braised lamb shanks, preheat oven to 180C. Heat oil in a large frying pan over medium-high heat, season shanks to taste, add to the pan in batches and cook, turning once, until browned all over (2-3 minutes each side). Transfer to a casserole with remaining ingredients, bring to a simmer, cover with a lid and braise in the oven until meat is falling from the bone (3-3¼ hours). Set shanks aside, skim fat from braising liquid, then reduce over medium heat until slightly thickened (30-40 minutes). Return shanks to braising sauce and keep warm.

2 Scatter parmesan over a large oven tray lined with baking paper and bake until golden and crisp (8 minutes). Roast almonds on a separate oven tray until golden (6-8 minutes). Cool parmesan and almonds, then transfer both to a food processor and process until finely chopped.

3 Heat a char-grill pan over medium-high heat, add leeks and grill, turning occasionally, until completely blackened (15-20 minutes). Transfer to a large bowl, cover with plastic wrap and steam until tender (2-3 minutes). Remove with tongs (reserve juices) and discard blackened layer.

4 Add zucchini, herbs, lemon juice, oil and sugar to bowl with leek juices, season to taste, and stir gently to combine. Just before serving, stir in parmesan and almond crumbs. Serve shanks hot with braising sauce, burnt leeks and zucchini salad.

WINE SUGGESTION An elegant nebbiolo.

252 GOURMET TRAVELLER | MENUS

FROM LEFT:
JEFF BENNETT,
CHRIS SORRELL,
MARK LABROOY,
DARREN ROBERTSON
& SAM REID-BOQUIST

APRÈS-SKI WITH THE THREE BLUE DUCKS

APRÈS-SKI WITH THE THREE BLUE DUCKS

BEEF CHEEKS WITH RADISH, MUSTARD SEED AND PICKLED CELERY SALAD

"This dish also goes really well with soft polenta," says Robertson. "For best results, don't be afraid to really caramelise the cheeks before braising – this will make a huge difference to the result." Begin this recipe a day ahead to pickle the celery.

PREP TIME 1 HR, COOK 3 HRS 50 MINS (PLUS COOLING, PICKLING)
SERVES 6

—

- 1½ tbsp olive oil
- 6 beef cheeks (280gm each)
- 1.5 litres (6 cups) veal stock
- 100 ml shiraz
- 1 carrot, coarsely chopped
- 1 white onion, coarsely chopped
- 2 garlic cloves, crushed
- 3 juniper berries
- 1 cinnamon quill
- ½ long red chilli
- 1 fresh bay leaf
- 1 thyme sprig
- 1½ tbsp yellow mustard seeds
- 6 baby radishes, shaved on a mandolin
- 2 tbsp coarsely chopped flat-leaf parsley

PICKLED CELERY
- 6 coriander seeds
- 100 ml rice wine vinegar
- 2 tsp caster sugar
- 2 celery stalks, stringy parts removed, cut into 4cm batons
- 2 tsp lime juice

BURNT ONION PURÉE
- 4 red onions, unpeeled, trimmed, halved
- 1 tbsp olive oil
- 2 Desiree potatoes (360gm), peeled and thickly sliced
- 20 gm butter, coarsely chopped
- 2 tsp lime juice

1 For pickled celery, dry-roast coriander seeds until fragrant (30-40 seconds; see cook's notes p279), then reduce heat to medium, add vinegar and sugar, stir to dissolve sugar, then set aside to cool. Add celery and lime juice, then refrigerate for 24 hours to pickle.

2 Preheat oven to 180C. Heat 2 tsp oil in a large frying pan over medium-high heat, season beef to taste and cook in batches, turning once, until browned (1-2 minutes each side). Transfer beef to a casserole, add stock, wine, carrot, onion, garlic, juniper berries, cinnamon, chilli, bay leaf and thyme, cover with a lid and braise in oven until very tender (3 hours). Remove beef and keep warm. Strain liquid into a saucepan, reserving 375ml (discard solids), and simmer to reduce to a thick sauce consistency, then keep warm.

3 Meanwhile, for burnt onion purée, place onions on an oven tray lined with baking paper, drizzle with oil, season to taste, roast until completely caramelised (40-50 minutes), then set aside to cool. When cool enough to handle, remove skin (discard), transfer to a saucepan, add potato, cover with reserved braising liquid and 375ml water, and simmer over medium heat until all liquid evaporates (30-40 minutes). Transfer to a food processor, blend until smooth, add butter and lime juice, season to taste and stir to combine.

4 Cook mustard seeds in a small saucepan of simmering water to remove bitterness (1-2 minutes), then drain, transfer to a bowl, add radish, parsley, drained pickled celery, 20ml pickling juice and remaining olive oil and season to taste.

5 Divide burnt onion purée among plates, top with beef cheeks, spoon a little reduced braising liquid over, top with radish, mustard seed and pickled celery salad and serve.

DRINK SUGGESTION A porter such as Bright Staircase.

RICE PUDDING

"This pudding also works well for breakfast with yoghurt, poached fruit and lots of cups of coffee," says Robertson.

PREP TIME 20 MINS, COOK 1 HR 20 MINS
SERVES 6

—

100 gm (½ cup) black quinoa (see note)
200 gm (1 cup) black glutinous rice (see note)
Juice and finely grated rind of 2 oranges
4 cloves
2 each star anise and cinnamon quills
1.5 litres (6 cups) milk
600 ml pouring cream
2 vanilla beans, split, seeds scraped
120 gm brown sugar
1½ tbsp each chia seeds, linseed and pumpkin seeds (see note)
Caster sugar, to taste

1 Dry-roast quinoa in a wide saucepan over low-medium heat for 1 minute, add black rice and dry-roast for 30 seconds, then add orange juice and rind and spices and simmer until juice evaporates (2-3 minutes). Add milk, cream, vanilla beans and seeds and a pinch of salt and bring to a simmer. Reduce heat to low and stir occasionally until rice is tender (1 hour). Add brown sugar and cook until rice is very tender and not too wet (15 minutes).
2 Meanwhile, dry-roast chia seeds, linseed and pumpkin seeds in a frying pan over medium heat (1-2 minutes).
3 Stir seeds into rice mixture, transfer to bowls, scatter with caster sugar, caramelise with a blowtorch or under a hot grill and serve.
NOTE Black quinoa, black glutinous rice, chia seeds, linseed and pumpkin seeds are available from select health-food shops.
WINE SUGGESTION A fruity moscato.

APRÈS-SKI WITH THE THREE BLUE DUCKS

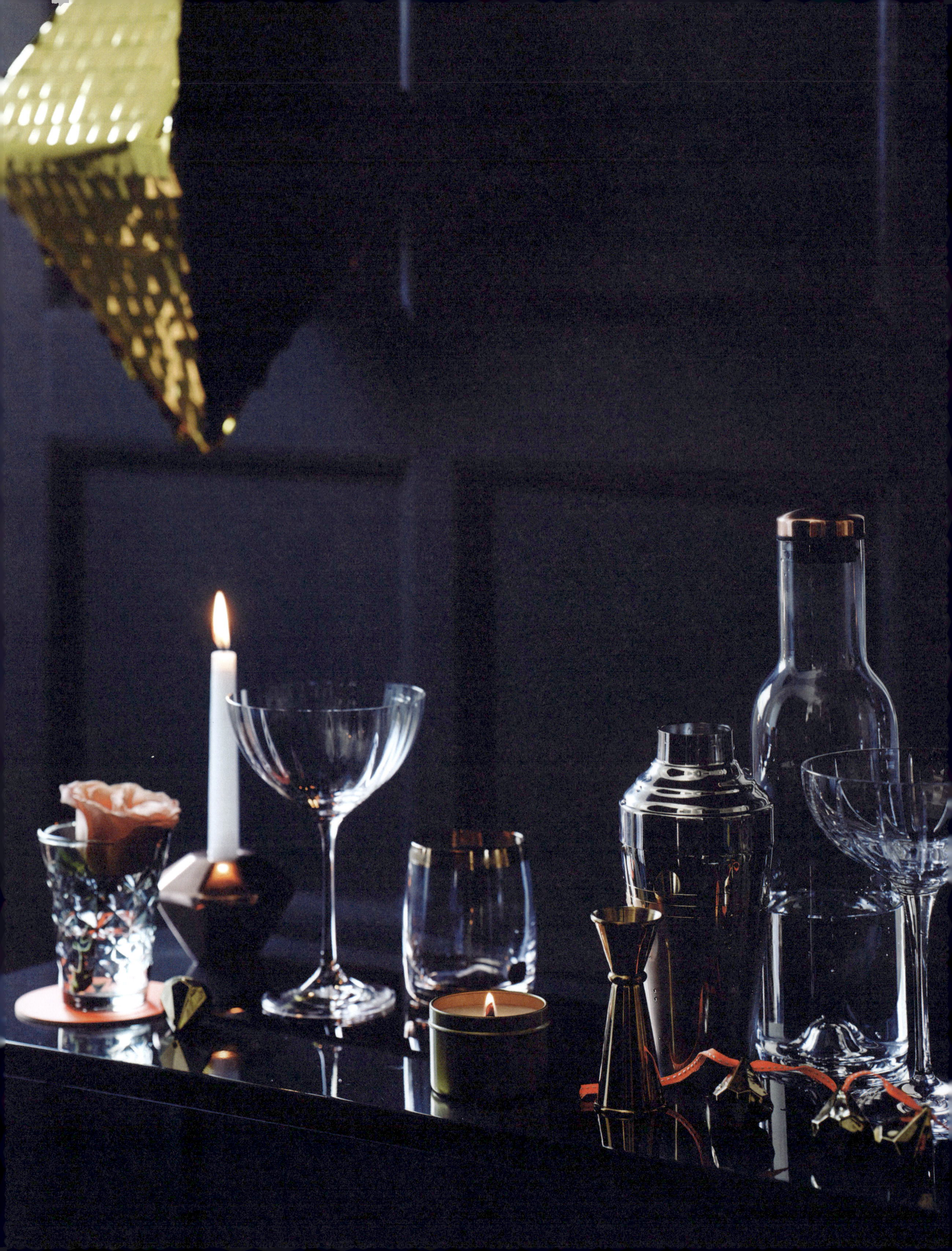

COCKTAIL HOUR

With smart finger food at the ready and cool cocktails to match, you've got the makings of a swell party. Start planning your next soirée with these fun ideas. Fried mortadella and provolone sandwiches are just the beginning.

—

+ Grilled baby corn with spiced salt and whipped feta

+ Scallop tartare and sea urchin toasts

+ Mozzarella with mint dressing and crostini

+ Cured kingfish with seaweed

+ Potato, pork and Sichuan pepper pastries

+ Fried mortadella sandwiches

+ *Amaro and Rye*
+ *Sherry Cobbler*
+ *Ruby Crush*
+ *Umeshu Cooler*

—

GRILLED BABY CORN WITH SPICED SALT AND WHIPPED FETA

Baby corncobs in their husks can be found at farmers' markets; otherwise use regular baby corn. The accompaniments would work just as well with full-sized corn at a summer lunch.

PREP TIME 15 MINS, COOK 10 MINS
SERVES 6-8

—

36 baby corn, preferably in the husk
Extra-virgin olive oil, to serve
SPICED SALT
1 tsp fennel seeds
½ chipotle chilli (4gm), thinly sliced
Finely grated rind of ¼ lime
WHIPPED FETA
140 gm Persian feta, drained
1 tbsp lime juice
Extra-virgin olive oil, to serve

1 For spiced salt, dry-roast fennel seeds and chipotle in a small frying pan until toasted and fragrant (20-30 seconds; see cook's notes p279). Transfer to a mortar and pestle and pound to a fine powder, then add 3 tsp salt flakes and lime rind and pound to combine.
2 For whipped feta, blend ingredients in a food processor until smooth. Transfer to a serving bowl and drizzle with extra-virgin olive oil.
3 Char-grill corn in batches over high heat, turning occasionally (3-5 minutes). Keep warm in a low oven while you repeat with remaining corn. Serve with spiced salt and whipped feta.

SHERRY COBBLER

PREP TIME 5 MINS
MAKES 1

—

2 thick slices orange, quartered
1 tsp caster sugar, or to taste
60 ml manzanilla sherry
60 ml freshly squeezed orange juice
Seasonal fruit, such as orange slices, and pineapple leaves, to garnish

1 Muddle orange slices and sugar in a Boston glass or cocktail shaker, then add sherry, orange juice and ice cubes. Cover and shake vigorously, then strain into a glass over fresh ice, garnish with fruit and a pineapple leaf and serve.

COCKTAIL HOUR

COCKTAIL HOUR

SCALLOP TARTARE AND SEA URCHIN TOASTS

Any thinly shaved sashimi-grade fish works nicely here in place of the scallop meat.

PREP TIME 20 MINS, COOK 10 MINS
SERVES 6-8

---

36 thin baguette slices
    Olive oil, for brushing
1 garlic clove, halved
300 gm scallop meat, very thinly sliced
20 gm salted capers, rinsed and coarsely chopped
2 tbsp finely chopped coriander
1 tsp extra-virgin olive oil, plus extra for brushing
    Tabasco and coriander cress, to serve
SEA URCHIN MAYO
70 gm sea urchin roe (see note)
2 tbsp lemon juice
150 ml mild-flavoured olive oil

1 For sea urchin mayo, blend roe and lemon juice in a small food processor until combined, then, with motor running, add olive oil in a thin steady stream until emulsified and a thick mayonnaise forms. Season to taste.
2 Preheat a grill to high. Brush baguette slices with olive oil and grill until toasted (1-2 minutes each side), then rub with cut garlic.
3 Mix scallop meat, capers and coriander in a bowl, then drizzle with olive oil, season to taste with ground pepper and Tabasco, and mix to combine.
4 Spoon a little sea urchin mayo onto each toast, top with scallop mixture and coriander cress and serve.
NOTE Sea urchin roe is available from select fishmongers. You may need to order it ahead.

RUBY CRUSH

PREP TIME 5 MINS
MAKES 1

---

45 ml dry gin
45 ml freshly squeezed ruby grapefruit juice
15 ml Campari
    Chilled soda water, to serve
    Thinly sliced ruby grapefruit, to serve

1 Pour gin into a well-chilled tumbler, then add grapefruit juice and Campari and stir to combine. Add a slice of grapefruit, top with soda water and crushed ice, and serve.

MOZZARELLA WITH MINT DRESSING AND CROSTINI

Buffalo mozzarella mixed with a little crème fraîche makes a wonderful creamy dip; if you've got some great burrata to hand, it makes a delicious alternative, but you may want to omit the cream.

PREP TIME 15 MINS, COOK 5 MINS
SERVES 6-8

—

- 2 buffalo mozzarella balls (about 130gm each), drained at room temperature
- 2 tbsp crème fraîche
- 1 tbsp pouring cream
- 1 tbsp lemon juice
- 2 tbsp thinly sliced mint
- Smoked paprika, to serve
- Extra-virgin olive oil, to serve

SEEDED CROSTINI
- ½ seeded baguette (150gm-200gm), thinly sliced
- Olive oil, for brushing
- 1 garlic clove, halved

1 For crostini, heat a char-grill pan over high heat. Brush bread with olive oil and grill, turning once, until golden (1-2 minutes each side), then rub with cut garlic.

2 Break mozzarella into a large shallow serving bowl. Combine crème fraîche with cream and lemon juice and season to taste, then drizzle mixture over mozzarella, top mozzarella with mint and smoked paprika to taste, drizzle with extra-virgin olive oil and serve with crostini.

COCKTAIL HOUR

COCKTAIL HOUR

CURED KINGFISH WITH SEAWEED

Any fresh seaweed (or soaked and sliced wakame) works nicely as the garnish here. Start this recipe a day ahead to cure the kingfish.

PREP TIME 20 MINS
SERVES 6-8

—

400 gm piece daikon, thickly sliced crossways
100 gm fresh seaweed rinsed and thinly sliced (see note)
Finely grated rind of 1 lemon and 1 orange
Baby shiso leaves, to serve (see note)
Toasted sesame seeds, to serve

CURED KINGFISH
500 gm piece skinned sashimi-grade kingfish
2 tbsp sea salt flakes
1 tbsp caster sugar
1 large piece konbu, rehydrated in hot water for 1 hour, drained

SESAME DRESSING
1 tbsp light soy sauce
3 tsp brown rice vinegar
1 tsp roasted sesame oil
½ tsp wasabi

1 For cured kingfish, place kingfish in a non-reactive container (see cook's notes p279), mix salt and sugar in a bowl, then scatter mixture evenly over both sides of kingfish and cover with the konbu. Refrigerate overnight to cure. Rinse and pat dry with paper towels.
2 For sesame dressing, whisk ingredients in a bowl until well combined.
3 Cut kingfish into 3cm cubes. Arrange daikon rounds on a platter, top each with a cube of kingfish, then seaweed, scatter with rind, shiso and sesame seeds, drizzle with dressing and serve.
NOTE Fresh seaweed is available from select fishmongers and Asian grocers. Baby shiso is available from farmers' markets and select greengrocers.

UMESHU COOLER

This cocktail goes particularly well with the kingfish appetiser above.

PREP TIME 5 MINS
MAKES 1

—

45 ml umeshu (see note)
15 ml sweet vermouth
15 ml freshly squeezed lemon juice
1 thin slice ginger, bruised
Strip of lemon peel, to serve

1 Combine umeshu, sweet vermouth, lemon juice and ginger in a shaker filled to three-quarters with ice. Stir for a minute, then strain into a tumbler with fresh ice (discard ginger). Garnish with lemon peel.
NOTE Umeshu is a sake-based liqueur made with the ume fruit; we've used Ota Shuzo "Dokan", an umeshu available from blackmarket.com.au.

POTATO, PORK AND SICHUAN PEPPER PASTRIES

It's really important to use fresh Sichuan peppercorns for the best flavour, so buy a fresh packet. These pastries can be made ahead and refrigerated, ready to be fried just before serving. They could also be fried beforehand and reheated in a warm oven.

PREP TIME 30 MINS, COOK 35 MINS
MAKES 20

—

- 600 gm Desiree potatoes (about 3), peeled and diced
- 2 tbsp vegetable oil or lard
- 1 small onion, finely chopped
- 100 gm mild pancetta, finely diced
- 1 tbsp Sichuan peppercorns, coarsely ground with a mortar and pestle
- ⅓ cup coarsely chopped coriander
- Vegetable oil, for deep-frying

LARD PASTRY
- 100 gm lard, melted and cooled
- 200 gm (1⅓ cups) self-raising flour
- 250 gm (1⅔ cups) plain flour

SICHUAN SALT
- 1 tbsp Sichuan peppercorns
- 1 tbsp sea salt flakes

1 For lard pastry, combine lard, flours, 160ml cold water and a pinch of fine sea salt in a bowl, and knead until a smooth dough forms. If dough is too sticky, add a little extra flour. Cover with plastic wrap and stand to rest for 30 minutes.

2 Boil potatoes in a large saucepan of salted water until tender (6-10 minutes). Drain and set aside uncovered to steam dry (10 minutes).

3 Meanwhile, heat oil in a frying pan over medium-high heat, add onion and pancetta and sauté, stirring occasionally, until onion is very tender and translucent (8-10 minutes). Add Sichuan pepper and stir until fragrant (1-2 minutes), then add potato, stir until potato has absorbed the pan fat, then add coriander, season to taste with salt and cool.

4 Divide pastry into 20 even pieces. On a lightly floured surface, halve each piece, then roll each half to an 8cm-diameter round. Place a scant tablespoonful of potato mixture in the centre of one round, cover with the other round, press edges together to seal, then carefully lift the edges and pleat around in one direction to secure. Place on a lightly floured tray and repeat with remaining dough and potato mixture.

5 Heat vegetable oil in a deep-fryer or deep saucepan to 180C. Add pastries in batches and fry, turning occasionally, until golden (4-6 minutes; be careful, hot oil will spit). Drain on paper towels.

6 For Sichuan salt, pound the peppercorns and salt with a mortar and pestle. Serve pastries warm sprinkled with Sichuan salt to taste.

COCKTAIL HOUR

COCKTAIL HOUR

FRIED MORTADELLA SANDWICHES

These little sandwiches can be made and fried ahead; just pop them in the oven when it's time to serve to warm them through and melt the cheese.

PREP TIME 30 MINS, COOK 20 MINS
MAKES 36

—

400 gm butter, diced
Dijon mustard, for spreading
18 slices light rye bread
18 thin slices mortadella (400gm)
Dill pickles, thinly sliced (optional), to serve
18 slices provolone dolce (360gm)

1 Make clarified butter by heating butter in a saucepan over low heat until fat separates from milk solids (20-30 minutes). Skim impurities from the top with a spoon, then strain the liquid butter into a clean container until you reach the milky solids on the base (discard these). The butter should be free of impurities; if some remain, strain the butter through a piece of fine muslin. Clarified butter will keep for 3 weeks stored in an airtight container in the refrigerator.
2 Spread mustard over half the bread slices, then top with mortadella and pickles, then the provolone and season to taste. Sandwich with remaining bread, then trim off crusts and set aside.
3 Preheat oven to 200C. Heat 2 tbsp clarified butter in a large frying pan over high heat, add 2 sandwiches and fry, turning once, until golden (2-3 minutes each side). Transfer to a board and repeat with remaining butter and sandwiches. Carefully slice each sandwich into 4 finger sandwiches and transfer to an oven tray lined with baking paper.
4 To serve, bake finger sandwiches until cheese melts (4-6 minutes) and serve warm.

AMARO AND RYE

PREP TIME 5 MINS
MAKES 1

—

1 pitted fresh cherry
30 ml Amaro Montenegro
30 ml rye whiskey
1 tsp freshly squeezed lemon juice
Fresh or jarred morello cherry, to garnish

1 Muddle cherry in a Boston glass or cocktail shaker, then add remaining ingredients except garnish, fill with plenty of ice and shake until well chilled. Strain into a chilled glass, add a cherry and serve.

INDEX

A

AÏOLI
Potato aïoli 25

ALMONDS
Ajo blanco 250
Roasted carrots with feta, almonds
　　　and sherry caramel 233

APPLES
Apple and candied ginger self-saucing
　　　pudding 217
Baked apples with burnt cream 151
Winter slaw 183

APRICOTS
Apricots poached in orange muscat with
　　　mascarpone and almonds 97

ASPARAGUS
Asparagus with caper and shallot butter 93

B

BANANAS
Golden pavlova with mango yoghurt
　　　and tropical fruits 63

BARBECUED DISHES
Char-grilled corn 18
Cider-brined smoked turkey with cranberry
　　　barbecue sauce 128
Grilled chicken with pickled
　　　watermelon salad 60
Grilled marron on a stick with citrus
　　　butter, flowers and herbs 225
Grilled shiitake mushrooms with
　　　umami butter 234
Grilled wagyu rump cap 229
Smoky eggplant and pomegranate salad 44
Swordfish with agrodolce sauce 89
Wood-fired rib-eye with jaew, butter
　　　lettuce and Asian herbs 78
Xinjiang-style lamb skewers 160

BARLEY
Rabbit broth with rabbit and
　　　barley dumplings 175
Salt-baked pumpkin with Pyengana
　　　cream and toasted grains 226

BARRAMUNDI
Steamed barramundi, chilli black beans
　　　and pickled mustard greens 163

BEEF
Beef cheeks with radish, mustard seed
　　　and pickled celery salad 255
Beef rib roast with beetroot
　　　and horseradish 212
Green peppercorn beef with caraway cream 131
Grilled wagyu rump cap 229
Roast beef with buttermilk 90
Wood-fired rib-eye with jaew, butter
　　　lettuce and Asian herbs 78

BEETROOT
Beef rib roast with beetroot and horseradish ... 212
Beetroot soup with burrata 100
Crostini with smoked eel pâté and
　　　glacé beetroot 35
Dill-cured rainbow trout with beetroot
　　　and potato cakes and fresh
　　　horseradish 178

BLUEBERRIES
Blueberry cobbler with lemon
　　　curd cream 26

BONE MARROW
Peará sauce 199

BONITO
Bonito with mojama 109

BROCCOLINI
Broccolini with chilli and burnt-garlic
　　　vinaigrette 148

BUCKWHEAT
Mushrooms and grains 250

BUTTERMILK
Bonito with mojama 109
Fried rabbit 142
Roast beef with buttermilk 90

C

CABBAGE
Winter green salad 237
Winter slaw 183

CAKES
Burnt honey madeleines 119
Sponge cake 238

CARAMEL
Crème caramel 238
Hot caramel and star anise milk 218
Salted-caramel semifreddo 152

CARAWAY
Green peppercorn beef with
　　　caraway cream 131

CARROTS
Carrots with garlic, ginger, spring onion
　　　and smoked chilli butter 214
Cauliflower salad with orange and cumin
　　　dressing, and buffalo yoghurt 132
Roast carrots with honey, sesame
　　　and parmesan 145
Roasted carrots with feta, almonds and
　　　sherry caramel 233
Smoked trout, Dutch carrots and
　　　butter sauce 247
Winter slaw 183

CAULIFLOWER
Cauliflower salad with orange and cumin
　　　dressing, and buffalo
　　　yoghurt 132

CAVOLO NERO
Rabbit broth with rabbit and barley
　　　dumplings 175
Winter green salad 237

CELERIAC
Celeriac and Gruyère fritters 172

CELERY
Beef cheeks with radish, mustard seed
　　　and pickled celery salad 255
Celery salt 104
Crab and celery mayonnaise on crostini 87
Roast quail with yoghurt and celery 104
Smoky chestnut soup 222

CEVICHE
Kingfish ceviche with young coconut
　　　and lime 53

CHEESE
Beetroot soup with burrata 100
Celeriac and Gruyère fritters 172
Grilled baby corn with spiced salt and
　　　whipped feta 260
Fried mortadella sandwiches 271
Mozzarella with mint dressing
　　　and crostini 264
Onion and bacon soup with mustard and
　　　cheese crust 206
Roasted carrots with feta, almonds and
　　　sherry caramel 233
Roast pumpkin with radicchio, ricotta salata,
　　　chilli and lemon 113
Salt-baked pumpkin with Pyengana cream
　　　and toasted grains 226
Tomato and bread salad 94
Tomato salad with feta and basil 21

CHERRIES
Amaro and Rye 271
Cherry lattice pie with almond-milk ice 135
Chocolate and Turkish coffee granita
　　　with poached cherries 47

CHESTNUTS
Chestnut "worms" with all sorts
　　　of mushrooms 182
Smoky chestnut soup 222

CHICKEN
Grilled chicken with pickled watermelon salad ... 60
Loudogg's twice-cooked crisp-skinned chicken ... 79
Roast spatchcock with garlic-bread sauce ... 149
White-cut chicken, aromatic chilli oil and peanuts ... 167

CHICORY
Winter green salad ... 237

CHOCOLATE
Chocolate and Turkish coffee granita with poached cherries ... 47
Quince, pecan and crème caramel trifle with Gretchen's honey cream ... 238

CLAMS
Clambake ... 25
Clam chowder ... 15

COCONUT
Coconut sorbet ... 81
Nama sea pearls ... 69
Turmeric and coconut salmon curry ... 72

COFFEE
Affogato "my style" ... 81
Chocolate and Turkish coffee granita with poached cherries ... 47
Tiramisù ... 202

CORN
Char-grilled corn ... 18
Chilled corn soup with yabbies ... 122
Grilled baby corn with spiced salt and whipped feta ... 260

CRAB
Crab and celery mayonnaise on crostini ... 87
Fujian-style scallop and spanner crab fried rice ... 164

CRANBERRIES
Cranberry barbecue sauce ... 128

CROSTINI
Crab and celery mayonnaise on crostini ... 87
Crostini with smoked eel pâté and glacé beetroot ... 35
Mozzarella with mint dressing and crostini ... 264

CUCUMBER
Cucumber pickle ... 57
Smoky eggplant and pomegranate salad ... 44

CURRIES
Turmeric and coconut salmon curry ... 72

CUSTARD
Crème caramel ... 238
Pouring custard ... 185

D

DESSERTS
Affogato "my style" ... 81
Apple and candied ginger self-saucing pudding ... 217
Apricots poached in orange muscat with mascarpone and almonds ... 97
Baked apples with burnt cream ... 151
Blueberry cobbler with lemon curd cream ... 26
Caramelised pineapple with green Sichuan peppercorn ice-cream ... 168
Cherry lattice pie with almond-milk ice ... 135
Chocolate and Turkish coffee granita with poached cherries ... 47
Goat's yoghurt sorbet with warm burnt honey madeleines ... 119
Golden pavlova with mango yoghurt and tropical fruits ... 63
Hot cross cannoli ... 201
Parsnip puddings ... 185
Quince, pecan and crème caramel trifle with Gretchen's honey cream ... 238
Rice pudding ... 256
Salted-caramel semifreddo ... 152
Tiramisù ... 202

DRINKS
Amaro and Rye ... 271
Dark and Stormy ... 12
Enoteca Tonic ... 32
Hot caramel and star anise milk ... 218
Pineapple, Mint, Ginger and Lime Crush ... 86
Ruby Crush ... 263
Sherry Cobbler ... 260
Sparkling passionfruit cordial ... 50
Umeshu Cooler ... 267

DUMPLINGS
Rabbit broth with rabbit and barley dumplings ... 175

E

EEL
Crostini with smoked eel pâté and glacé beetroot ... 35

EGGPLANT
Smoky eggplant and pomegranate salad ... 44

EGGS
Devilled Easter eggs ... 188
Egg and vegetable fried rice ... 75

F

FENNEL
Slow-roasted pork shoulder with fennel ... 183

FINGER LIMES
Kingfish ham ... 191

FISH AND SEAFOOD
Bonito with mojama ... 109
Chilled corn soup with yabbies ... 122
Clambake ... 25
Clam chowder ... 15
Crab and celery mayonnaise on crostini ... 87
Crostini with smoked eel pâté and glacé beetroot ... 35
Cured kingfish with seaweed ... 267
Dill-cured rainbow trout with beetroot and potato cakes and fresh horseradish ... 178
Fujian-style scallop and spanner crab fried rice ... 164
Gin-cured ocean trout with herb crust ... 57
Grilled marron on a stick with citrus butter, flowers and herbs ... 225
Kingfish ceviche with young coconut and lime ... 53
Kingfish ham ... 191
Lobster tagliarini ... 39
Roast oysters with horseradish ... 138
Scallops with brown-bread butter and pancetta ... 54
Scallop tartare and sea urchin toasts ... 263
Scampi "casino" ... 192
Smoked trout, Dutch carrots and butter sauce ... 247
Swordfish with agrodolce sauce ... 89
Steamed barramundi, chilli black beans and pickled mustard greens ... 163
Turmeric and coconut salmon curry ... 72

FRITTERS
Celeriac and Gruyère fritters ... 172

G

GARLIC
Beef rib roast with beetroot and horseradish ... 212
Broccolini with chilli and burnt-garlic vinaigrette ... 148
Carrots with garlic, ginger, spring onion and smoked chilli butter ... 214
Potato aïoli ... 25
Roast spatchcock with garlic-bread sauce ... 149
Scampi "casino" ... 192

GINGER
Carrots with garlic, ginger, spring onion and smoked chilli butter ... 214
Dark and Stormy ... 12
Pineapple, Mint, Ginger and Lime Crush ... 86

GOAT'S MILK
Goat's yoghurt sorbet with warm burnt honey madeleines ... 119

GRAPEFRUIT
Enoteca Tonic ... 32
Ruby Crush ... 263

H

HAM
Pea and ham salad ... 125

HONEY
Burnt honey madeleines ... 119
Quince, pecan and crème caramel trifle with Gretchen's honey cream ... 238
Roast carrots with honey, sesame and parmesan ... 145

HORSERADISH
Beef rib roast with beetroot and horseradish ... 212
Roast oysters with horseradish ... 138

I

ICE-CREAMS & ICES
Almond-milk ice ... 135
Chocolate and Turkish coffee granita ... 47
Coconut sorbet ... 81
Goat's yoghurt sorbet ... 119
Green Sichuan peppercorn ice-cream ... 168
Salted-caramel semifreddo ... 152

J

JERUSALEM ARTICHOKES
Jerusalem artichoke chips ... 159
Parsnip and artichoke soup ... 244

K

KALE
Winter green salad ... 237

KINGFISH
Cured kingfish with seaweed ... 267
Kingfish ceviche with young coconut and lime ... 53
Kingfish ham ... 191

KOHLRABI
Winter slaw ... 183

L

LAMB
Braised lamb shanks, burnt leeks and zucchini salad ... 251
Slow-roasted lamb with citrus and herbs ... 110
Spicy lamb cigars in brik pastry ... 36
Xinjiang-style lamb skewers ... 160

LEEKS
Braised lamb shanks, burnt leeks and zucchini salad ... 251
Leeks with green sauce ... 116
Potato and leek salad with mustard dressing ... 58

LEMONS
Citrus butter ... 225
Lemon curd cream ... 26
Slow-roasted lamb with citrus and herbs ... 110

LIMES
Citrus butter ... 225
Pineapple, Mint, Ginger and Lime Crush ... 86

LOBSTER
Lobster tagliarini ... 39

M

MADELEINES
Burnt honey madeleines ... 119

MANGOES
Golden pavlova with mango yoghurt and tropical fruits ... 63

MARRON
Grilled marron on a stick with citrus butter, flowers and herbs ... 225

MASCARPONE
Tiramisù ... 202

MILK
Hot caramel and star anise milk ... 218

MINT
Mozzarella with mint dressing and crostini ... 264
Pea and ham salad ... 125
Pickled watermelon salad ... 60
Pineapple, Mint, Ginger and Lime Crush ... 86
Roast pumpkin with radicchio, ricotta salata, chilli and lemon ... 113

MORTADELLA
Fried mortadella sandwiches ... 271

MOZZARELLA
Mozzarella with mint dressing and crostini ... 264

MUSHROOMS & OTHER FUNGI
Chestnut "worms" with all sorts of mushrooms ... 182
Chinese mushrooms with warrigal greens and Jerusalem artichokes ... 159
Grilled shiitake mushrooms with umami butter ... 234
Mushrooms and grains ... 250
Pearà sauce ... 199
Pickled black fungus ... 156

MUSSELS
Clambake ... 25

N

NECTARINES
Nectarine salad ... 44

O

OCEAN TROUT
Gin-cured ocean trout with herb crust ... 57

OLIVES
Braised rabbit with sauce ... 199

ONIONS
Beef cheeks with radish, mustard seed and pickled celery salad ... 255
Burnt onion purée ... 255
Onion and bacon soup with mustard and cheese crust ... 206

ORANGES
Candied orange peel ... 32
Citrus butter ... 225
Orange and cumin dressing ... 132
Pineapple, Mint, Ginger and Lime Crush ... 86
Sherry Cobbler ... 260
Slow-roasted lamb with citrus and herbs ... 110

OYSTERS
Roast oysters with horseradish ... 138

P

PANCETTA
Potato, pork and Sichuan pepper pastries ... 268
Scallops with brown-bread butter and pancetta ... 54
Scampi "casino" ... 192

PARSNIPS
Parsnip and artichoke soup ... **244**
Parsnip puddings ... **185**

PASSIONFRUIT
Golden pavlova with mango yoghurt and tropical fruits ... **63**
Sparkling passionfruit cordial ... **50**

PASTA
Chestnut "worms" with all sorts of mushrooms ... **182**
Lobster tagliarini ... **39**

PASTRIES
Hot cross cannoli ... **201**
Potato, pork and Sichuan pepper pastries ... **268**
Spicy lamb cigars in brik pastry ... **36**

PASTRY
Cinnamon pastry ... **135**
Lard pastry ... **268**

PÂTÉ
Crostini with smoked eel pâté and glacé beetroot ... **35**

PAVLOVA
Golden pavlova with mango yoghurt and tropical fruits ... **63**

PEARS
Radish, pear and seaweed salad with miso dressing ... **209**

PEAS
Pea and ham salad ... **125**

PECANS
Quince, pecan and crème caramel trifle with Gretchen's honey cream ... **238**

PICKLES
Cucumber pickle ... **57**
Pickled celery ... **255**
Pickled watermelon rind ... **60**

PIES
Cherry lattice pie with almond-milk ice ... **135**

PINEAPPLE
Caramelised pineapple with green Sichuan peppercorn ice-cream ... **168**
Golden pavlova with mango yoghurt and tropical fruits ... **63**
Pineapple, Mint, Ginger and Lime Crush ... **86**

PORK
LP nachos ... **68**
Roast shoulder of pork ... **43**
Slow-roasted pork shoulder with fennel ... **183**

POTATOES
Burnt onion purée ... **255**
Chestnut "worms" with all sorts of mushrooms ... **182**
Dill-cured rainbow trout with beetroot and potato cakes and fresh horseradish ... **178**
Goose-fat roast potatoes with dukkah ... **213**
Potato aïoli ... **25**
Potato and leek salad with mustard dressing ... **58**
Potato, pork and Sichuan pepper pastries ... **268**
Smoked potatoes ... **116**

PRAWNS
Clambake ... **25**

PUDDINGS
Apple and candied ginger self-saucing pudding ... **217**
Blueberry cobbler with lemon curd cream ... **26**
Parsnip puddings ... **185**
Rice pudding ... **256**

PUMPKIN
Roast pumpkin with radicchio, ricotta salata, chilli and lemon ... **113**
Roast pumpkin with thyme and lemon butter, and spiced seeds ... **129**
Salt-baked pumpkin with Pyengana cream and toasted grains ... **226**

Q

QUAIL
Roast quail with yoghurt and celery ... **104**

QUINCE
Quince, pecan and crème caramel trifle with Gretchen's honey cream ... **238**

QUINOA
Rice pudding ... **256**
Salt-baked pumpkin with Pyengana cream and toasted grains ... **226**

R

RABBIT
Braised rabbit with sauce ... **199**
Fried rabbit ... **142**
Rabbit broth with rabbit and barley dumplings ... **175**

RADICCHIO
Roast pumpkin with radicchio, ricotta salata, chilli and lemon ... **113**

RADISHES
Beef cheeks with radish, mustard seed and pickled celery salad ... **255**
Radish, pear and seaweed salad with miso dressing ... **209**

RAINBOW TROUT
Dill-cured rainbow trout with beetroot and potato cakes and fresh horseradish ... **178**
Smoked trout, Dutch carrots and butter sauce ... **247**

RICE
Anchovy fried rice ... **198**
Egg and vegetable fried rice ... **75**
Fujian-style scallop and spanner crab fried rice ... **164**
Rice pudding ... **256**
Salt-baked pumpkin with Pyengana cream and toasted grains ... **226**

ROCKET
Potato and leek salad with mustard dressing ... **58**

ROCKMELON
Kingfish ham ... **191**

S

SALADS
Cauliflower salad with orange and cumin dressing, and buffalo yoghurt ... **132**
Nectarine salad ... **44**
Pea and ham salad ... **125**
Pickled celery salad ... **255**
Pickled watermelon salad ... **60**
Potato and leek salad with mustard dressing ... **58**
Radish, pear and seaweed salad with miso dressing ... **209**
Roasted carrots with feta, almonds and sherry caramel ... **233**
Smoky eggplant and pomegranate salad ... **44**
Tomato and bread salad ... **94**
Tomato salad with feta and basil ... **21**
Winter green salad ... **237**
Winter slaw ... **183**
Zucchini salad ... **251**

SALMON
Turmeric and coconut salmon curry 72

SALT
Celery salt 104
Salt-crust dough 226
Sichuan salt 268
Spiced salt 260

SANDWICHES
Fried mortadella sandwiches 271

SCALLOPS
Fujian-style scallop and spanner
 crab fried rice 164
Scallops with brown-bread butter
 and pancetta 54
Scallop tartare and sea urchin toasts 263

SCAMPI
Scampi "casino" 192

SEAWEED
Cured kingfish with seaweed 267
Grilled shiitake mushrooms with
 umami butter 234
Nama sea pearls 69
Radish, pear and seaweed salad with
 miso dressing 209

SMOKED TROUT
Smoked trout, Dutch carrots
 and butter sauce 247

SORREL
Winter green salad 237

SOUPS
Beetroot soup with burrata 100
Chilled corn soup with yabbies 122
Clam chowder 15
Onion and bacon soup with mustard
 and cheese crust 206
Parsnip and artichoke soup 244
Rabbit broth with rabbit and
 barley dumplings 175
Smoky chestnut soup 222

SPATCHCOCK
Roast spatchcock with garlic-bread sauce 149

SPECK
Anchovy fried rice 198
Onion and bacon soup with mustard
 and cheese crust 206

SPELT
Mushrooms and grains 250
Pickled watermelon salad 60

SPINACH
Winter green salad 237

SWORDFISH
Swordfish with agrodolce sauce 89

T

TERRINE
Pressed veal head terrine 103

TOMATOES
Lobster tagliarini 39
Smoky eggplant and pomegranate salad 44
Tomato and bread salad 94
Tomato salad with feta and basil 21

TRIFLE
Quince, pecan and crème caramel trifle
 with Gretchen's honey cream 238
Tiramisù 202

TURKEY
Cider-brined smoked turkey with cranberry
 barbecue sauce 128

TURNIPS
Smoky chestnut soup 222

V

VEAL
Pressed veal head terrine 103

W

WATERMELON
Pickled watermelon rind 60
Pickled watermelon salad 60

Y

YABBIES
Chilled corn soup with yabbies 122

YOGHURT
Cauliflower salad with orange and cumin
 dressing, and buffalo yoghurt 132
Goat's yoghurt sorbet with warm burnt
 honey madeleines 119
Golden pavlova with mango yoghurt
 and tropical fruits 63
Roast quail with yoghurt and celery 104

Z

ZUCCHINI
Anchovy fried rice 198
Braised lamb shanks, burnt leeks and
 zucchini salad 251
Zucchini salad 251

ZUCCHINI FLOWERS
Sautéed zucchini flowers with lemon,
 chilli and garlic 24

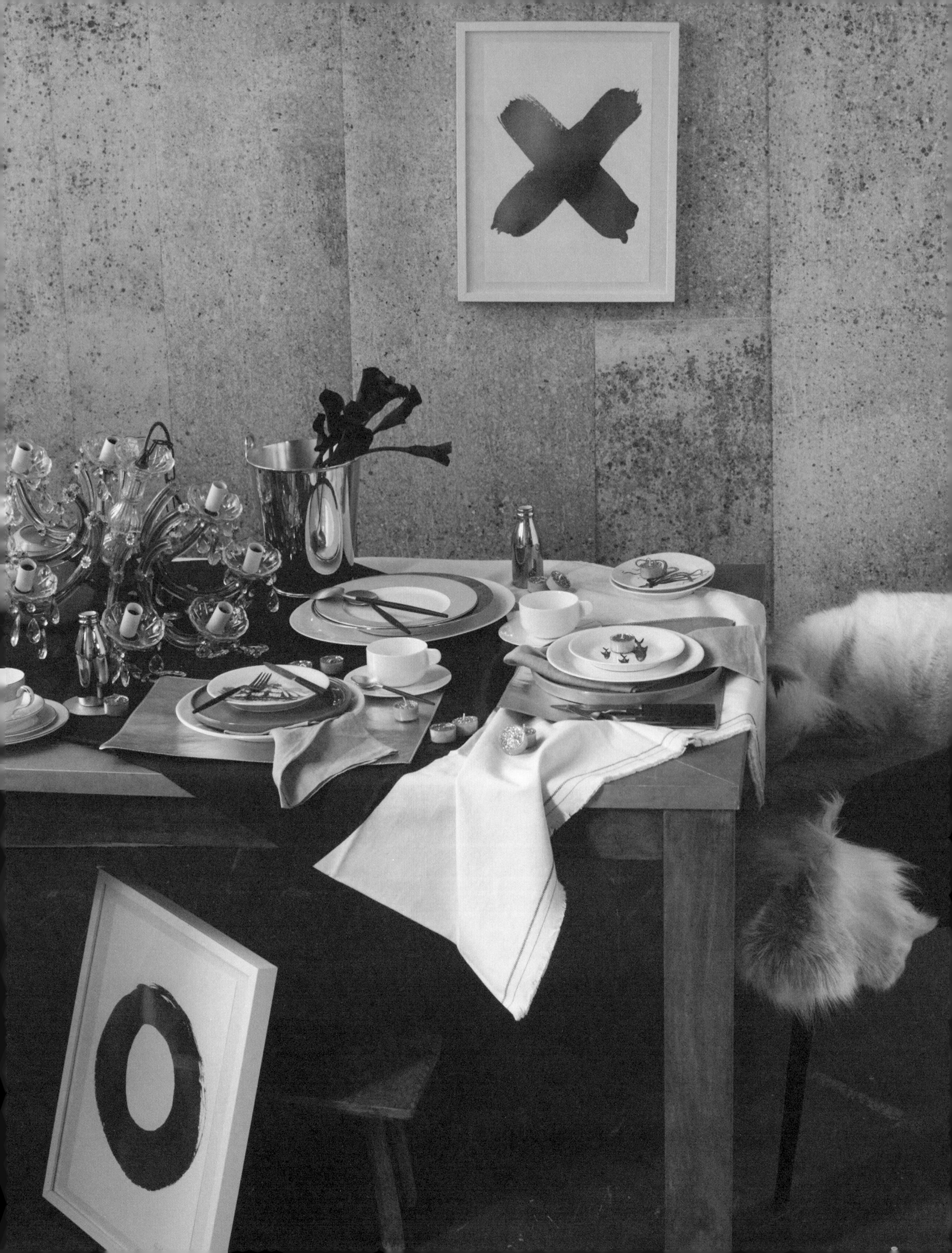

COOK'S NOTES

MEASURES & EQUIPMENT

+ All cup and spoon measures are level and based on Australian metric measures.
+ Eggs have an average weight of 59gm unless otherwise specified.
+ Fruit and vegetables are peeled and medium-sized unless otherwise specified.
+ Oven temperatures are for conventional ovens and need to be adjusted for fan-forced ovens.
+ Pans are medium-sized and heavy-based, and cake tins are stainless steel, unless otherwise specified.

COOKING TIPS

+ When seasoning food to taste, we use sea salt and freshly ground pepper unless otherwise specified.
+ To blanch an ingredient, cook it briefly in a large saucepan of boiling water. To refresh it, plunge it in plenty of iced water. This stops the cooking process.
+ We recommend using free-range eggs, chicken and pork. We use female pork, not male.
+ To dry-roast spices, cook the spices in a dry pan over medium-high heat, stirring continuously, until they're fragrant. The cooking time varies depending on the spices used.
+ RSPCA Australia's recommendations for killing crustaceans humanely are to first render the animals insensible by placing them in the freezer (under 4C – signs of insensibility are when the tail or outer mouth parts can be moved without resistance); crustaceans must then be killed quickly by cutting through the centreline of the head and thorax with a knife. For crabs, insert a knife into the head. This splitting and spiking destroys the nerve centres of the animal.
+ All herbs are fresh, and both leaves and tender stems are used, unless otherwise specified.
+ Non-reactive bowls are made from glass, ceramic or plastic. Use them in preference to metal bowls when marinating to prevent the acid in marinades reacting with metal and imparting a metallic taste.
+ Eggwash is lightly beaten egg unless otherwise specified, used for glazing or sealing.
+ Sugar syrup is made of equal parts caster sugar and water, unless otherwise specified. Bring the mixture to the boil to dissolve the sugar, remove it from the heat and cool it before use.
+ Acidulated water is a mixture of water and lemon juice; it prevents discolouration.
+ To sterilise jars and lids, run them through the hot rinse cycle in a dishwasher, or wash them in hot soapy water, rinse well, place on a tray in a cold oven and heat at 120C for 30 minutes.
+ To blind-bake, line a pastry-lined tart tin with baking paper, then fill it with weights (ceramic weights, rice and dried beans work best).
+ To test whether marmalade, jam or jelly has reached setting point, you'll need a chilled saucer (place a couple in the freezer before you start cooking). Remove the pan from the heat, spoon a little mixture onto the saucer and return it to the freezer for 30 seconds, then draw your finger through the mixture – it should leave a trail, indicating that the mixture has reached setting point. If not, cook for another few minutes before testing again. If you prefer, use a sugar thermometer to measure when the mixture reaches 105C; once it does, you can begin testing for setting point.
+ To clarify butter, cook it over low heat until the fat and milk solids separate. Strain off the clear butter and discard the milk solids. You will lose about 20 per cent of the volume in milk solids.

ACKNOWLEDGEMENTS

It's been a great pleasure working with the chefs, photographers, writers, sommeliers and stylists whose talent, voice and vision are featured in these pages. Thank you for being part of Gourmet Traveller.

—

BONDI CLAMBAKE
Recipes Tom Walton
Photography Ben Dearnley
Styling Vanessa Austin and Emma Knowles
Drink suggestions Max Allen

CHRISTMAS FEAST
Recipes Brigitte Hafner
Photography John Laurie
Styling Lisa Featherby
Drink suggestions James Broadway

LUNCH BY THE BEACH
Recipes Emma Knowles and Alice Storey
Photography William Meppem
Styling Emma Knowles, Alice Storey and Vanessa Austin
Drink suggestions Max Allen

HOLLYWOOD DINNER PARTY
Recipes and drink suggestions Louis Tikaram
Photography William Meppem
Styling Emma Knowles

SMART-CASUAL LUNCH
Recipes Emma Knowles and Lisa Featherby
Photography Anson Smart
Styling Emma Knowles and Geraldine Muñoz
Drink suggestions Max Allen

LUNCH IN PARIS
Recipes James Henry and Shaun Kelly
Photography William Meppem
Styling Emma Knowles and Élodie Rambaud
Drink suggestions Max Allen

CHRISTMAS ALFRESCO
Recipes Alice Storey
Photography Chris Court
Styling Claire Delmar and Alice Storey
Drink suggestions Max Allen

EASTER AT ESTER
Recipes and drink suggestions Mat Lindsay
Photography Ben Dearnley
Styling Emma Knowles

LEE HO FOOK'S ASIAN BANQUET
Recipes Victor Liong
Photography Sharyn Cairns
Styling Lisa Featherby
Drink suggestions Masa Nishimoto

BLUE MOUNTAINS HARVEST LUNCH
Recipes Sean Moran
Photography Ben Dearnley
Styling Lisa Featherby
Drink suggestions Matt Hardy

EASTER AT 10 WILLIAM ST
Recipes Daniel Pepperell
Photography Ben Dearnley
Styling Lisa Featherby
Drink suggestions Matt Young

FIRESIDE SUPPER
Recipes Rodney Dunn
Photography William Meppem
Styling Rodney Dunn & Emma Knowles
Drink suggestions Max Allen

SUNDAY LUNCH WITH PETER GILMORE
Recipes Peter Gilmore
Photography Ben Dearnley
Styling Lisa Featherby
Drink suggestions Russ Mills and Amanda Yallop

APRÈS-SKI WITH THREE BLUE DUCKS
Recipes Shannon Debreceny, Mark LaBrooy and Darren Robertson
Photography William Meppem
Styling Lisa Featherby
Drink suggestions Shannon Debreceny and Jeff Bennett

COCKTAIL HOUR
Recipes Lisa Featherby
Photography Mark Roper
Styling Lisa Featherby and Lynsey Fryers-Hedrick

Still life photography Hugh Stewart